SAMSON DAUDA

SAMSON DAUDA

Biography

The Road to Bodybuilding Greatness

El Spiritus

SAMSON DAUDA

Copyright © El Spiritus, 2024

All rights reserved.

No part of this publication may be reproduced, distributed, or transmitted in any form or by any means, including photocopying, recording, or other electronic or mechanical methods, without the prior written permission of the publisher, except in the case of brief quotations embodied in critical reviews and certain other noncommercial uses permitted by copyright law.

SAMSON DAUDA

TABLE OF CONTENTS

INTRODUCTION
CHAPTER 1: Early Life and Beginnings
The Foundations of Discipline
First Steps into Fitness
Discovering the World of Bodybuilding
The Influence of Early Role Models
CHAPTER 2 : The Path to Professionalism
Making the Decision to Compete
Training with Purpose: Early Lessons
Overcoming Initial Setbacks
CHAPTER 3: The Breakthrough Moment
Stepping Onto the National Stage
A Defining Win: Turning Points in His Career
Rising in the Rankings
Gaining Recognition in the Bodybuilding Community
CHAPTER 4: Building a Championship Physique

SAMSON DAUDA

Perfecting Muscle Mass and Symmetry
Tailoring His Diet for Maximum Growth
Tailoring His Diet for Maximum Growth
The Role of Supplementation in His Success
CHAPTER 5: Mindset of a Champion
Mental Toughness in the Face of Challenges
Staying Focused on Long-Term Goals
Dealing with Competition Pressure
Visualising Success: Samson's Mental Strategies
CHAPTER 6: Competing at the Elite Level
Qualifying for International Competitions
The Experience of Competing on the Olympia Stage
Learning from Rival Competitors
Balancing Fame and Focus
CHAPTER 7: The Role of Support Systems
Family, Friends, and Personal Relationships
The Importance of Coaches and Mentors

Sponsorships and Industry Partnerships

Fans and Community: How They Fuel His Success

CHAPTER 8: Challenges Along the Way

Injury and Recovery: Overcoming Setbacks

Dealing with Self-Doubt and Fear

Navigating the Politics of the Bodybuilding Industry

The Battle with Consistency and Motivation

CHAPTER 9: Inspiring the Next Generation of Athletes

Giving Back to the Bodybuilding Community

Expanding His Brand Beyond Bodybuilding, Shaping the Future of the Sport

CHAPTER 10: Looking Forward

Future Goals: Beyond the Stage

Life After Competition: What's Next for Samson Dauda?

The Evolution of His Training and Philosophy

SAMSON DAUDA

<u>CONCLUSION</u>

INTRODUCTION

Samson Dauda's journey to bodybuilding greatness is a story about dedication, perseverance, and a commitment to self-improvement. Samson's rise from humble beginnings to being one of the best in the world of professional bodybuilding shows how a true champion is made. His story is about a mindset that has allowed him to push beyond personal limits and social expectations. Samson Dauda was born in Nigeria and raised in the UK, but it wasn't until later in life that he became interested in bodybuilding. Like many people in the sport, his first steps were filled with uncertainty. He had to deal with competition, self-doubt, and the challenge of building a body that could compete on the world stage. Samson is special because he always wants to get stronger and more defined, but also because he does it with precision and skill. Samson's path was challenging at first. Bodybuilding is hard work both mentally and physically. Competitors train hard, perfect their diets,

SAMSON DAUDA

and keep a high level of discipline that leaves little room for error. Samson used this challenge as a driving force. He used every obstacle as a learning experience, from his first local competition to the national stage. Each moment helped him grow as an athlete and as a person. But what makes Samson so successful is not just his natural talent or work ethic, but also his mindset. His focus on the mental aspects of the sport—staying motivated, visualising success, and overcoming moments of doubt—has been just as important to his rise as his time in the gym. Samson Dauda created a plan to be successful that combines physical, mental, and emotional elements. This book will tell the story of Samson Dauda's life, including his early struggles, important moments in his career, and how he has influenced bodybuilding. Through his story, we learn what it takes to reach the top of one of the most demanding sports in the world.

SAMSON DAUDA

CHAPTER 1: Early Life and Beginnings

Samson Dauda started his career in Lagos, Nigeria, where he was born on April 8, 1992. Dauda grew up in Lagos, Africa's biggest city, where bodybuilding was not a popular sport. As a child, Dauda was naturally athletic and enjoyed many physical activities. But it wasn't until his teenage years that he discovered his love for weightlifting and bodybuilding. He became interested in bodybuilding magazines and videos, which introduced him to the world of muscular bodies and competitive posing. Dauda started exercising in a humble way. Like many people who want to become bodybuilders in places with limited resources, he started training with whatever equipment was available. This required him to make do with everyday items and basic weights. Even with these limitations, his dedication and natural talent for the sport quickly became clear. Dauda started exercising more seriously in gyms in Lagos when he was in his twenties. It was during this time that he started to get attention for his outstanding physical development and potential. His quick progress caught the attention of more experienced

SAMSON DAUDA

bodybuilders and trainers in the area who saw his potential and gave him advice. Dauda kept getting stronger and learning.

Balancing his studies and his growing passion for bodybuilding presented challenges, but it also taught him a strong work ethic and time management skills that would help him in his future career. The young Nigeria's first competitions came in local and regional bodybuilding shows in Nigeria. Even though these early competitions were small compared to what he would do later, they helped Dauda become more confident and comfortable on stage. They helped me understand how to prepare for a competition, how to pose, and how to think well while competing. Dauda's success at local competitions inspired him to pursue bodybuilding at a higher level. However, he faced numerous challenges. The bodybuilding scene in Nigeria was still growing, and there were few opportunities for international competition. Additionally, launching a bodybuilding career in Nigeria presented significant challenges. Dauda continued to train hard and look for opportunities to show off his physique. He started to make a name for himself in the African bodybuilding scene. His performances in regional competitions attracted attention not only in Africa but also from international bodybuilding circles. As Dauda's fame grew, so did his dreams of competing on the global stage. He started to look into ways to train and compete internationally, which would eventually lead him to move to the United Kingdom. This move marked a turning point in his career, opening new opportunities for training, nutrition, and competition. Samson Dauda was very perseverant and passionate about bodybuilding. Dauda started bodybuilding in Lagos and became famous internationally. His story demonstrates how people from diverse backgrounds can enjoy bodybuilding.

The Foundations of Discipline

The Samson Dauda approach to bodybuilding is characterised by an extraordinary level of discipline that has become legendary in the professional bodybuilding community. Early years in Nigeria cultivated his

SAMSON DAUDA

disciplined mindset, which he refined as he progressed through his career, laying the foundation for his success in the sport. Dauda's training philosophy is the starting point for his discipline. He is known for his methodical approach to workouts and keeps to his training schedules. His training usually involves high-volume workouts that often include up to 20–25 sets per body part. This shows not only physical strength but also mental fortitude to keep the intensity up during long sessions. Dauda is known for his focus and attention to details. He focuses on proper form and mind-muscle connection over simply moving heavy weights. This disciplined approach to technique has helped him build his signature physique while reducing the risk of injury. The Nigerian-born bodybuilder's discipline goes beyond the gym walls and into his nutrition. Dauda follows a strict diet year-round. His off-season nutrition plan usually includes 6–8 meals a day, carefully measured and timed to help him reach his training goals. To eat healthy, plan and prepare it. This can take hours each week. Dauda demonstrates her organisational skills during competition preparation. He is known for

SAMSON DAUDA

following his diet plan exactly and measuring all his food carefully. His ability to stick to his nutrition plan, even when faced with the extreme hunger that often comes with contest prep, has earned him respect from his peers and coaches. Dauda's discipline includes resting and recovering.

Despite his rigorous workouts and hard work, Dauda still manages to get enough sleep every night. He usually gets 8–9 hours. This commitment to recovery shows that he knows that discipline isn't just about pushing harder but also about knowing when to rest and recover. Dauda's disciplined lifestyle includes time management. He plans his days carefully to fit in his training, meals, rest periods, and other obligations. This way of organising helps him prepare well and handle the many responsibilities of being a professional athlete. Dauda's mental discipline is very important. He thinks about bodybuilding as a long-term goal because he knows that it takes years of hard work to become successful in the sport. This way of thinking helps him stay focused during positive and bad times in his career. It prevents

SAMSON DAUDA

him from feeling happy or discouraged when things are going well. In bodybuilding, posing practice is crucial, and Dauda shows discipline. He spends a lot of time perfecting his posing routines, knowing that it's just as important to show off his body on stage as it is in the gym. His careful preparation shows that he knows what it takes to do well at the highest level. Social media posts and behind-the-scenes footage often showcase Dauda's discipline. His commitment to the process is always clear. However, he asserts that discipline entails consistency and the ability to correct course when circumstances falter. In interviews, Dauda often talks about how his upbringing in Nigeria influenced his disciplined approach to bodybuilding. The challenges he faced in a country with limited resources taught him the importance of making the most of every opportunity and never taking anything for granted. This background has taught him the importance of discipline in achieving his goals. His training partners and coaches often comment on how dedicated he is to his preparation. Even when many bodybuilders might relax their standards, Dauda keeps his disciplined approach. He understands that sustained consistency is the foundation for true success in bodybuilding. Professional bodybuilder Samson Dauda has always maintained discipline. From training and nutrition to recovery and mental preparation, his methodical and dedicated approach has become a blueprint for success in the sport.

First Steps into Fitness

Samson Dauda's first steps into fitness began in Lagos, Nigeria, where he learned about weight training and physical development. Dauda started exercising when he was a teenager. Like many young athletes in Nigeria, he started exercising without much equipment. He used things he found and weights he made to do his exercises. This approach to training helped him build strength and prepare for his future in bodybuilding. He started doing weight training at local gyms in Lagos, but the equipment was old and not as effective as modern gyms. These gyms gave Dauda his first real chance to learn about resistance training. The limited resources available helped him focus on basic movements and proper form

SAMSON DAUDA

instead of using sophisticated machinery. As Dauda started to take fitness more seriously, he learned about training principles through whatever resources he could find. He read magazines about bodybuilding, watched training videos, and asked experts at his gym for advice. He learned exercise science and training methods by himself. His body changed a lot in the beginning, even though he didn't have much information or money. His natural ability to build muscle became apparent as his body responded well to basic training protocols. This early success made him want to exercise more seriously and eventually led him to compete in bodybuilding. During this time, Dauda tried different ways of training and found what worked best for him. He started to build his training philosophy, which stressed the importance of consistency and proper form over lifting heavy weights without purpose. At first, maintaining a healthy diet was challenging due to limited options and insufficient information.

Dauda had to rely on local foods to help him reach his training goals. This experience taught him valuable

SAMSON DAUDA

lessons about using what's available and how important it is to eat well for physical growth. His first training programs focused on compound movements, which would later become the cornerstone of his training philosophy. He started with basic exercises like squat, deadlift, and bench press. The community aspect of fitness influenced Dauda's early development. He discovered other fitness enthusiasts in Lagos who assisted him in initiating his bodybuilding journey. These early relationships helped shape his understanding of training and gave him valuable encouragement during his formative years in the sport. Dauda started to incorporate more advanced training principles into his workouts. He learned that it's important to work muscles slowly, take breaks and rest, and use different training methods to build muscles and make them stronger. As Dauda grew, she became a bodybuilder. Others in the local fitness community recognized his potential for competitive bodybuilding. Dauda's first steps into fitness, while humble, set the foundation for the patterns and principles that would later define his approach to professional bodybuilding. During this time, he faced many difficulties, like not having much equipment and not knowing much about food. This experience instilled in him a strength and determination that would prove invaluable in his future career.

Discovering the World of Bodybuilding

Samson Dauda discovered bodybuilding and became very interested in fitness. He became very passionate about being physically good. He was introduced to competitive bodybuilding through bodybuilding magazines and videos. When Dauda started learning about bodybuilding, he became interested in the bodies of famous bodybuilders in these books. He studied their training methods, poses, and competition preparations, taking in as much information as he could about this type of athletic development. This period of discovery helped him understand what was possible through dedicated training and proper nutrition. Dauda began to understand the differences between general fitness training and bodybuilding-specific protocols. He learned about the importance of muscle isolation exercises, the role of

SAMSON DAUDA

proper nutrition in growing muscles, and the specific requirements of contest preparation. This knowledge changed his training approach from basic strength work to more focused bodybuilding. Despite the small sample size, Dauda competed in bodybuilding in Nigeria. He attended local shows and competitions and learned about the various aspects of competition, from posing routines to stage presence. These experiences helped him want to compete and made him want to take bodybuilding more seriously. Dauda attempted bodybuilding training for the first time, encountering both challenges and achievements. He started focusing on muscle hypertrophy and symmetry instead of just strength gains. As he adjusted to these new training methods, his innate ability to build muscle became increasingly apparent. He had to make big changes in how he trained, from general fitness to bodybuilding workouts.

He learned to control movements through all ranges of motion and target specific muscle groups with different exercises. During this time, he learned how to train in a way that became his favourite. Dauda realised that

SAMSON DAUDA

excellent nutrition was very important for bodybuilding success. He learned about macronutrients, meal times, and the specific dietary requirements for building and maintaining muscle mass. Even though Nigerian foods were limited, he worked to improve his nutrition. Dauda learned that it's important to pose when bodybuilding. He spent a lot of time doing poses and talking in gyms. He learned how to pose early on, and it helped him later in his career. The community aspect of bodybuilding influenced Dauda's growth during this time. He met other bodybuilders in Lagos and shared his knowledge and experiences, which helped him learn more about the sport. These relationships helped him achieve his bodybuilding goals. As he learned more about bodybuilding, he became more interested in the artistic parts of the sport. Dauda began to understand that bodybuilding was not just about building muscle but about creating a physique that was balanced in size, symmetry, and conditioning. This knowledge changed how he trained and helped him set goals for the sport in the future. The discovery phase also introduced Dauda to bodybuilding's mental aspects. He learned about the importance of discipline, consistency, and mental toughness in sports. These lessons would be invaluable as he went from an aspiring competitor to a professional athlete. Dauda's early competitions at local shows gave him practical experience in the competitive aspects of bodybuilding. These events, which were smaller than international competitions, helped him understand the preparation process, stage presentation, and mental challenges of competing. Each competition gave him valuable lessons that helped him become a bodybuilder. As he learned more about bodybuilding, Dauda started to set higher goals for himself in the sport. He started to think about competing at higher levels and possibly making bodybuilding a career. During this time, he learned important things that helped him become successful in the sport. Through this process of discovering bodybuilding, Dauda learned about what it would take to succeed in the sport at a high level. He learned a lot during this time, and it helped him become a professional bodybuilder.

The Influence of Early Role Models

SAMSON DAUDA

Samson Dauda became a bodybuilder because of his role models, who inspired and guided him. Magazines and videos of famous competitors first introduced Dauda to bodybuilding in Nigeria. Ronnie Coleman, the eight-time Mr. Olympia champion, was one of Dauda's most significant early influences. Coleman's work ethic and training approach drew Dauda to his combination of size and conditioning. Coleman's training sessions and his famous "Yeah buddy!" and "Light weight!" mantras became sources of motivation for Dauda during his own rigorous workouts. Dorian Yates, who won Mr. Olympia six times, helped Dauda learn how to train. Yates' high-intensity training philosophy and emphasis on form over weight influenced Dauda's training method. Yates' training principles in various bodybuilding publications helped Dauda understand proper training techniques and the importance of intensity in workouts. Phil Heath's training and presentation impressed Dauda. Dauda's approach to muscle refinement and symmetry influenced how Heath would later approach his own physique development. The seven-time Mr. Olympia's focus on developing a comprehensive package, encompassing

SAMSON DAUDA

everything from conditioning to stage presence, provided invaluable insights for bodybuilders. Local champions and experienced competitors inspired Dauda. Despite not being as famous as the Olympia champions, these athletes provided Dauda with advice and examples of what is achievable with hard work and limited resources. Dauda also liked Jay Cutler's business skills and professionalism in the sport. Dauda saw that bodybuilding could be more than just a competition. This influence helped Dauda understand the professional side of the sport.

These role models influenced more than just physical growth. Dauda studied how people interview, train, and prepare for competitions. He took in information about their nutrition strategies, recovery methods, and mental preparation techniques. Dauda's later success in the sport, especially his journey to become Mr. Olympia, inspired him as he pursued his own professional career. Curry showed Dauda that if she worked hard and took the right steps, she could do really well in sports. The way these champions behaved on and off stage

SAMSON DAUDA

influenced Dauda's professional behaviour. He learned what it meant to be a professional bodybuilder from their interactions with fans, fellow competitors, and the media. Dauda liked how Big Ramy became famous in bodybuilding because both athletes came from places that are not usually associated with successful bodybuilders. Ramy's success in becoming Mr. Olympia showed that geographical origins do not have to limit one's potential in the sport. Victor Martinez's famous body and style influenced Dauda's how she poses and looks on stage. Martinez's ability to show off his body by doing good poses helped Dauda understand how important it is to present yourself well when competing in bodybuilding. These role models influenced Dauda's training philosophy. He uses different methods but still has his own style. Their examples showed him how to succeed in the sport and helped him develop a good approach to bodybuilding. Dauda learned valuable lessons about perseverance through adversity, the importance of maintaining professionalism, and the need for continuous improvement. Their experiences, both successes and setbacks, gave him insights that would be

SAMSON DAUDA

useful in his own competitive career. Dauda's approach to the sport today continues to reflect these role models. They can be seen in his training methodology, attention to detail in preparation, and professional conduct on and off the competition stage. The lessons he learned from watching these great athletes have helped him become a professional bodybuilder and continue to help him grow in the sport. These early role models helped Dauda build his own unique approach to bodybuilding, combining traditional wisdom with innovative techniques to make his own path to success in the sport.

SAMSON DAUDA

CHAPTER 2 :The Path to Professionalism

Samson Dauda's journey to professional bodybuilding is a remarkable one. He started out in the amateur ranks and built his reputation through increasingly competitive shows. To become a professional bodybuilder, you had to do a lot of planning and work. Dauda started out in Nigeria and quickly became a top competitor. These early competitions were small, but they gave valuable experience in preparing for contests and speaking on stage. Dauda's move to the United Kingdom was important in her quest for professional status. This move gave us better places to train, food to eat, and job opportunities that weren't available in Nigeria. The move brought him together with experienced coaches and other athletes who would help him grow. Dauda competed in various federation shows during his amateur career. His performances at regional and national competitions showed that he was getting better with each show. These competitions helped him gain valuable experience and build his reputation in bodybuilding. The process of getting his pro card involved competing in qualifying shows sanctioned by the International Federation of Bodybuilding and Fitness (IFBB). Dauda worked carefully to win these contests, making sure that each time he won, he did better than before. His dedication to continually improving his physique and presentation skills became evident in his steadily improving placements. During this time, the training became more focused and sophisticated. Dauda worked with different coaches to find and fix his weaknesses. His workout routines evolved to incorporate more advanced techniques and principles, and his nutrition protocol became more precise and scientifically based. It was challenging to pursue a career in bodybuilding. Dauda had to balance his desire to compete with practical needs. He often worked to support his bodybuilding activities. This period required careful planning to cover the costs of training, nutrition, and competition.

SAMSON DAUDA

Dauda got better at preparing for competitions as she became a professional. He learned more about how his body responded to different approaches to diet and training, which allowed him to make more precise adjustments during contest prep. This helped a lot when there was more competition. Dauda learned a lot by connecting with people in the bodybuilding community. He built relationships with other competitors, coaches, and industry figures who gave him advice and opportunities. These connections helped him navigate the tough business world of professional bodybuilding. Dauda's IFBB Pro Card was a big step for his career, but it also meant a new challenge. The transition from amateur to professional competitor required changes in his approach, from training intensity to presentation standards. Dauda was new to the job and had to prove himself in a very competitive field. His early professional shows showed his potential but also showed areas that needed further development to compete at the highest levels. This period of adaptation saw him improve his approach while keeping the work ethic that had made him successful as an amateur. As Dauda

SAMSON DAUDA

became a pro bodybuilder, the business aspects of professional bodybuilding became more important. He started building a personal brand, connecting with sponsors, and using social media. These things were crucial for his job and helped him do well in competition. Working with supplement companies and equipment manufacturers helped him further his career. These relationships helped offset some of the costs associated with competing at the professional level while also giving him the chance to expand his influence in the industry. Dauda's training approach changed a lot during his transition to professional status. He worked out more and harder, and he paid more attention to how he prepared. Recovery protocols became more sophisticated and used different techniques to meet the demands of professional training. Meal plans became more precise and tailored to his specific needs. We carefully monitored and adjusted the quality and quantity of his nutritional intake to foster his growth and maintain his fitness for professional competition. The mental aspects of competing at the professional level required significant adjustment. Dauda made plans to handle the extra pressure and expectations that come with being a professional. This included working on his mental preparation and keeping focus during extended preparation periods. He got better at speaking when he competed in professional shows. Dauda worked with pose coaches to refine his stage presence. He was successful in his job because he paid close attention to how he spoke. Dauda learned to balance professional competition with other aspects of his career. The scheduling of training, meals, recovery, and business obligations required careful planning. Dauda kept in touch with his Nigerian bodybuilding roots while taking advantage of the opportunities in the international bodybuilding community. This combination of influences helped him become a professional competitor. To become a professional meant not only getting better physically but also growing as a person. Every step Dauda took helped him become an athlete and learn what it takes to be successful in bodybuilding.

Making the Decision to Compete

SAMSON DAUDA

Samson Dauda decided to compete in bodybuilding because of his natural talent, encouragement from others, and growing passion for the sport. The decision to move from casual training to competitive bodybuilding was a major turning point in his athletic journey. When he first started training in Nigeria, other gym members and trainers often commented on his outstanding genetic potential and rapid physical development. Dauda became interested in the sport and started thinking about competing. The decision-making process involved careful consideration of many different factors. Dauda looked at his physical abilities and compared them to other athletes he saw in magazines or videos. His big body and ability to build and keep muscle mass showed that he had the genes to be successful in sports. Local gym owners and bodybuilders in Lagos were important in encouraging Dauda to think about competing. They saw his potential and told him what it would be like to compete in bodybuilding. Their knowledge helped him understand the challenges and opportunities in bodybuilding competitions. Before entering a contest, Dauda learned how to prepare for it. He looked at the

SAMSON DAUDA

rules for different groups, weights, and clubs. This research phase facilitated his understanding of his potential fit in the competitive landscape and the necessary elements for success. He made his decision based on financial considerations. Bodybuilding necessitates significant financial investment in nutrition, supplements, training equipment, and competition expenses. Dauda had to figure out if he could afford to prepare for a competition while living in Nigeria. Another important thing to think about was how it would affect his personal life. To compete in bodybuilding, you need to dedicate a lot of time and change your lifestyle. Dauda had to balance these demands with his other obligations and relationships. Support from his immediate circle was important to his decision. Family and close friends helped him decide to pursue competitive bodybuilding. Dauda made her choice based on the timing. He chose to enter his first competition after building a solid foundation in training and nutrition. This plan helped him start competing when he was physically and mentally ready for the task. The availability of competitive opportunities in Nigeria influenced his initial competition choices. He began by participating in local shows, which were accessible and enjoyable without requiring significant financial investment. These early contests helped him see how talented he was at competing. Dauda also decided to compete because he saw successful African bodybuilders who had won international competitions. These athletes showed that geographical limitations need not prevent success in the sport, giving him inspiration for his own competitive aspirations. Preparing for his first competition helped him decide. As Dauda learned how to prepare for a competition, how to train and eat properly, and how mentally tough it is, he became more interested in competing. His first competitions were small, but they helped him see how good he could be at the sport. The judges' comments, how the audience liked him, and how he felt about himself made him decide to take bodybuilding competitions more seriously. Dauda decided to compete and wanted to learn more about it. He started learning how to prepare for a contest, how to pose, and how to present himself. This educational process helped him understand competitive bodybuilding and strengthen his commitment to the sport. The competitive environment gave him new motivation to train. Having specific goals and deadlines helped him focus his efforts and give his gym sessions more purpose. He liked how he prepared for competitions in a systematic way. Dauda started competing more often and realised he could do well in the sport. Each competition taught him lessons and experiences that helped him become more committed to bodybuilding. The decision to compete started a journey that would lead him to professional status. This initial choice to step on stage set the stage for his future achievements in the sport.

Training with Purpose: Early Lessons

Samson Dauda's early training experiences were characterised by a period of intense learning and adaptation as he discovered the most effective ways to build his physique. During his early years in Nigeria, his training methods changed from basic weightlifting to more advanced bodybuilding-specific protocols. Initially, Dauda primarily drew inspiration for his training sessions from magazines, videos, and the experiences of local gym veterans. He quickly learned that while basic movements were the foundation of his training, the execution and intent of each exercise were crucial for bodybuilding success. One of the most important early lessons was learning how important mind-muscle connection is. Instead of just moving weights from point A to point B, Dauda learned to feel each muscle work through its full range of motion. This principle became a cornerstone of his training philosophy and helped him grow quickly. Dauda learned valuable lessons from working with limited equipment in Nigerian gyms. He learned how to create effective workouts with basic equipment, focusing on exercise variations and techniques that stimulated muscles even without access to expensive machines. His early training required careful adjustment to volume and frequency. Dauda found out that his body responded well to higher-volume training, but the key was finding the right balance between stimulation and recovery. This understanding helped him design his approach to workout programming. During these early years, the significance

SAMSON DAUDA

of proper form became paramount. Dauda discovered that using heavier weights without proper form can lead to poor results and increase the risk of injury. This realisation led him to prioritise careful movements and good technique over excessive effort. Training partners helped Dauda's early development. Working with more experienced lifters helped him learn proper form, develop spotting techniques, and understand the importance of having someone push him during tough workouts. These partnerships also gave him valuable feedback about how he did things. Dauda's training method was based on overloading gradually. He learned how to increase the demands on his muscles by adding weight, increasing repetitions, or decreasing rest periods. This method of moving forward helped make sure that things got better over time. Another important lesson was that nutrition affects training effectiveness. Dauda found that his training results improved a lot when he ate well. This understanding led to more attention being given to pre- and post-workout nutrition.

SAMSON DAUDA

To train certain muscles well, he had to try different things and watch carefully. He learned that different body parts respond differently to different training techniques, rep ranges, and exercise choices. This knowledge helped him train body parts in a more balanced way. As Dauda trained harder, recovery became more important. He learned the importance of getting enough rest between workouts, getting enough sleep, and using active recovery methods. Knowing how muscle recovery affects muscle growth and development helped him train more often and harder. The idea of training splits emerged as an important part of his early development. Dauda tried different training splits to find the best way to structure his workouts while giving each muscle group enough recovery time. This process helped him figure out how to organise his training for the best results. Dealing with plateaus taught me how important it is to vary training. Dauda learned to change his workout routines when progress stopped. These experiences taught him the value of training with planned variation. During these early years, it became clearer how training affects the mind. Dauda developed strategies for staying focused during long workouts, pushing through tough sets, and staying motivated when progress was slow. These thinking skills were as important as physical abilities for his growth. Record-keeping became a key tool for keeping track of his training and making informed changes. Dauda started writing down his workouts, including how much weight he used, how many times he did each exercise, and how his body responded to different ways of training. This method of keeping track helped him find effective ways to train and areas that need improvement. Dauda learned to schedule efficient workouts. He learned that it's important to take breaks when needed, avoid distractions, and focus on exercises that are useful instead of doing things that don't work well. These early lessons helped Dauda become successful in bodybuilding later on. The principles and practices he developed during this period stayed with him as he progressed in the sport.

Overcoming Initial Setbacks

SAMSON DAUDA

Samson Dauda had some tough times when he started bodybuilding. These challenges were difficult, but they helped him learn how to build muscles and make him stronger. Dauda struggled to begin his career due to the lack of quality training available in Nigeria. Many gyms did not have modern equipment, and the available weights were often not enough for his growing strength. He had to change his training methods to work around equipment limitations. Another big problem was nutrition. In Nigeria, it was difficult and expensive to get the foods and supplements that bodybuilders usually use. Dauda had to learn to use locally available foods and often adapt traditional Nigerian meals to meet his nutritional needs. Early competitions had their own difficulties. Dauda faced disappointments in his first few shows. These initial competitive experiences revealed the need for him to enhance his physique and presentation, prompting him to reassess his approach to contest preparation. Injury management was a key learning experience during his early development. Dauda had to learn proper form and recovery techniques through trial and error. He learned that proper warm-up,

SAMSON DAUDA

form, and listening to his body's signals are important. During his early years, financial constraints posed ongoing challenges. Getting the right food, taking supplements, and competing was expensive, especially given the economic conditions in Nigeria. Dauda had to be careful with his resources, making sacrifices in other areas of his life to support his bodybuilding pursuits.

The lack of experienced mentors in his local area at first hampered his progress. Even though there were many experienced lifters in Nigerian gyms, few had competed at high levels in bodybuilding. Dauda had to study by himself and get help from people far away to improve his ability to compete. Another challenge was cultural beliefs about bodybuilding in Nigeria. Many people in his community didn't know or agree with how much he loved the sport. Despite occasional questions from those around him, Dauda maintained his focus and determination. Getting ready for competition was difficult at first. Issues with posing, presentation, and stage presence required a lot of work to overcome. He had trouble showing his body on stage, so he spent a lot

SAMSON DAUDA

of time learning how to pose properly. Dauda had to find a way to balance his training with other responsibilities. He had to make significant adjustments to his daily routine to accommodate multiple meals, workouts, and rest periods. Early setbacks tested his ability to bounce back. Competition results and plateaus in development took mental toughness to overcome. Dauda learned to use these experiences as motivation instead of letting them stop him from pursuing his goals. Getting to and from competitions was difficult for him when he started working. Travelling from Nigeria to international competitions involved a lot of planning and money. These logistical issues often made competition preparation more stressful. Learning how to prepare for a contest required some trial and error. Early attempts at competition prep sometimes led to missing his peak condition or dealing with unexpected challenges in the last weeks before a show. These experiences helped him develop a better approach to contest preparation. Language and communication barriers sometimes made it challenging to compete internationally or get advice from coaches abroad. Dauda had to work hard to overcome these obstacles to learn from and communicate with the broader bodybuilding community. Changing how judges judge different competitions required adjustments. It took time and experience to figure out what different federations and judges wanted. Every contest taught him how to prepare and present better. To keep progressing while dealing with different setbacks, you need to develop a resilient mindset. Dauda learned to see setbacks as opportunities to learn and improve, which would help him throughout his career. These early challenges helped Dauda develop as a bodybuilder. Each time he faced a challenge, he learned more about the sport and became more determined and strong.

Finding His First Coach and Team

Samson Dauda's journey to find a coach marked a big change in his bodybuilding career. After starting out training and getting help from local gym members in Nigeria, he decided to get professional coaching. This was a big step in his development as a competitive

SAMSON DAUDA

bodybuilder. Dauda started looking for coaches who could help her improve in the sport. His move to the United Kingdom opened new opportunities to connect with experienced coaches and established bodybuilding teams that could help him move to higher levels of competition. Nathan Harman was a significant influence on Dauda's early professional development. Harman helped Dauda improve how she trains and prepares for competitions. Under Harman's guidance, Dauda started to train and eat better. To become part of a formal training team, Dauda had to change how she trained before. His new coaches devised workout programs that emphasised the development of specific body parts while preserving his strongest features. Working with a professional team helped Dauda's nutrition plan become more organised. His coaches set meal times, macronutrient targets, and supplement protocols that were more precise than his previous self-directed efforts. This scientific approach to nutrition helped him build a better physique. His first coaching team went beyond just training and nutrition guidance. They also helped him improve his posing and presentation skills. This

SAMSON DAUDA

comprehensive approach to competition preparation greatly aided him in his competitive career. Communication is crucial in the relationship between a coach and athlete. Regular check-ins, progress photos, and detailed feedback sessions helped Dauda stay on track with his preparation while allowing him to adjust his program based on how his body responded. The team environment gave Dauda training partners who could push him in the gym. The presence of other bodybuilders aided in his development.

The coaching team helped Dauda fix specific weaknesses in his physique. Through targeted training approaches and careful attention to detail, they worked together to bring up lagging body parts and create better balance and symmetry. Working with his first coaching team was important because it taught him how to trust the process. Dauda had to follow structured programs and sometimes use approaches that were different from his previous methods. This trust in his coaches' expertise helped him see continued improvement. The team helped Dauda choose shows and make good peak-week strategies. Their experience in training athletes for competition helped him avoid common mistakes and improve his contest preparation. Dauda met people in the industry and other competitors by working with coaches. These connections helped him develop in the sport and assisted him better understand the professional bodybuilding landscape. The group of coaches established guidelines for improving and preventing injuries. Their bodybuilding experience helped Dauda maintain her progress while minimising the risk of injury or overtraining. The team helped Dauda understand the investments she needed to prepare for the competition. They gave advice on how to spend money on nutrition, supplements, and competition. His first coaching team became closer over time as they worked together to find the best ways to help him. This process of improving helped Dauda become successful in bodybuilding later on. Under professional guidance, documenting and tracking became more organised. His coaches kept detailed records of training sessions, nutrition, and progress measurements so they could make adjustments to the program. Working with his first coaching team

SAMSON DAUDA

was another important part. They helped Dauda understand how to structure his training and nutrition throughout the year to optimise his competition preparation while keeping long-term progress. His first coaching team helped him with more than just getting ready physically. They also helped him learn how to stay focused and deal with the pressures of competition.

SAMSON DAUDA

CHAPTER 3: The Breakthrough Moment

Samson Dauda became famous in bodybuilding after working hard for many years and being very dedicated to the sport. Dauda's path to success was neither straight-forward nor easy. He was born in Nigeria and later moved to the United Kingdom. He was not considered a natural-born athlete in bodybuilding at first, and like many others in the sport, he had to prove himself over time. His story is one of perseverance, dedication, and refusing to let circumstances or setbacks dictate his future. Dauda got better as he started bodybuilding, but it wasn't until he became an international bodybuilder that people noticed. His body was good, but he didn't look polished enough to do well in sports. For a long time, people thought Dauda had potential but wasn't ready to become a top athlete. But Dauda knew that the potential was not enough. He needed to work harder, perfect his posing, improve his conditioning, and find the right formula that would help him rise above the competition. The Arnold Classic marked Dauda's breakthrough moment. The Arnold

SAMSON DAUDA

Classic is a competition that attracts the best bodybuilders from all over the world. Winning it can lead to even bigger success in the sport. Dauda wanted to show that he was competent enough by attending this event. Dauda worked hard to prepare for the Arnold Classic. He knew that success would require more than just building muscle. He had to show a balanced and proportionate physique on stage, as well as perfect his stage presence and posing routine. These elements combined would determine whether he would be just another competitor or a true contender. When Dauda stepped on stage at the Arnold Classic, it was clear that something had changed. He was stronger and fitter than before. But the biggest difference was his confidence. Dauda finally found a place to show his best self, and the judges noticed. His performance was about the art of bodybuilding—the way he presented his body and the way he controlled it. When it comes to bodybuilding, especially at the highest levels, the difference between winning and losing can be the smallest details. Every pose, every movement, and any flaw can cost an athlete the top spot. Dauda was aware of this and took no

SAMSON DAUDA

chances. He performed the best he had ever done. Dauda was a strong and powerful person who looked right in every way. Dauda's moment under the lights was the culmination of years of hard work and sacrifice.

He made a big breakthrough that everyone in bodybuilding was excited about. Samson Dauda was now a legitimate contender, someone who had earned a place among the best in the sport. Dauda's reputation went up after his performance at the Arnold Classic. Fans and rivals started talking more about him. He had shown that he could compete at the highest level, and his future seemed brighter than ever. Dauda's triumph at the Arnold Classic transformed his career and unlocked previously closed doors for him. Dauda's breakthrough was not only physical but also mental and emotional growth. He was confident on stage because he had worked hard for years to build mental toughness and resilience. Dauda learned to handle both physical and mental aspects of bodybuilding. The discipline required to maintain the gruelling diet, training regimen, and lifestyle of a professional bodybuilder is immense, but

SAMSON DAUDA

Dauda embraced it fully. The man had a clear goal and was willing to work for it. This breakthrough moment was more than just winning a competition. It was about showing something to himself and the world. It was the realisation of a dream that had once seemed far away and impossible. Dauda believed he could do well in bodybuilding, and now he has proof. His success at the Arnold Classic made him one of the rising stars in the sport and set the stage for even greater success in the future. Samson Dauda's breakthrough moment shows how important it is to stay committed to a goal even when the path forward is uncertain. His climb to the top of bodybuilding was not easy, but he kept going because he believed in himself.

Stepping Onto the National Stage

Samson Dauda became one of the most promising athletes in bodybuilding slowly and steadily. His debut on the national stage marked a crucial point in his career. Dauda's story is one of passion, discipline, and the relentless pursuit of perfection. Stepping onto the

SAMSON DAUDA

national stage was a significant milestone in his development as a bodybuilder. Dauda was born in Nigeria and moved to the United Kingdom, where he would eventually begin his bodybuilding career. At first, he didn't focus on building muscles. Like many young athletes, he tried different sports, but once he discovered bodybuilding, he realised it was his true love. What started as a way to stay in shape quickly turned into a full-time career. Dauda wanted to turn his body into art and compete at the highest levels, so he worked hard both physically and mentally. Dauda started taking the sport seriously and worked on getting stronger. He also entered local competitions to gain experience. Early on, it was clear that he had a natural ability for bodybuilding and a genetic predisposition to size and shape that set him apart from many of his peers. But natural talent alone wasn't enough to get on the national stage. Dauda knew he had to improve his skills, get better at posing, and be ready for every competition. This meant paying attention to everything, from diet and training to recovery and stage presentation. Dauda's early successes at home caught the attention of people in the

SAMSON DAUDA

bodybuilding community. His physique was impressive; it showed a combination of size, symmetry, and aesthetics that showed his potential. It wasn't long before he started to get a following. People realised that he had what it took to compete at a higher level. People encouraged Dauda to focus on national competitions, where he would face the top bodybuilders in the country. Dauda was very excited to be on the national stage. Only the most disciplined and dedicated athletes emerge victorious in these competitions, showcasing their best talent. It was hard work preparing for his first national competition. Dauda knew he needed to work hard and get better so he could compete well in the UK.

This required modifying his diet, refining his workout routines, and ensuring he worked every muscle group to its maximum capacity. When Dauda became a national hero, he had an immediate impact. He brought a physique that combined mass and symmetry, a difficult balance in the sport of bodybuilding. His stage presence was strong, and his posing routine showed that he knew how to show off his strengths and minimise his

SAMSON DAUDA

weaknesses. Dauda's ability to show his physique in the best possible light is a skill that separates competent bodybuilders from great ones. Dauda worked hard to win the competition. He made a strong impression on the judges and got recognition for his overall development and presentation. Competing on the national stage not only raised Dauda's profile but also showed how hard he had worked. He was a national competitor with serious potential. Dauda's success on the national stage also changed how he approached sports. To do well at this level, he had to plan ahead and take care of himself throughout the year. National events require high conditioning and precise timing. Dauda had to learn how to build muscle in the off-season while getting lean and ready for competitions. Dauda approached this task with the same discipline and focus that had gotten him to this point. It was about showing himself and others that he could compete with the best. His performance in national competitions attracted a lot of attention from people in the business, sponsors, and other athletes. This exposure helped Dauda get the resources and support he needed to keep improving and reach bigger goals. Samson Dauda's entry onto the national stage was a big moment for his bodybuilding career. It was the result of years of hard work and dedication and also the beginning of his success in the sport. Dauda's ability to perform at a high level in these competitions showed that he had the potential to go even further, setting up his future success on the international bodybuilding scene.

A Defining Win: Turning Points in His Career

Samson Dauda became one of the most promising athletes in bodybuilding slowly and steadily. His debut on the national stage marked a crucial point in his career. Dauda's story is one of passion, discipline, and the relentless pursuit of perfection. Stepping onto the national stage was a significant milestone in his development as a bodybuilder. Dauda was born in Nigeria and moved to the United Kingdom, where he would eventually begin his bodybuilding career. At first, he didn't focus on building muscles. Like many young athletes, he tried different sports, but once he discovered bodybuilding, he realised it was his true love. What

SAMSON DAUDA

started as a way to stay in shape quickly turned into a full-time career. Dauda wanted to turn his body into art and compete at the highest levels, so he worked hard both physically and mentally. Dauda started taking the sport seriously and worked on getting stronger. He also entered local competitions to gain experience. Early on, it was clear that he had a natural ability for bodybuilding and a genetic predisposition to size and shape that set him apart from many of his peers. But natural talent alone wasn't enough to get on the national stage. Dauda knew he had to improve his skills, get better at posing, and be ready for every competition. This meant paying attention to everything, from diet and training to recovery and stage presentation. Dauda's early successes at home caught the attention of people in the bodybuilding community. His physique was impressive; it showed a combination of size, symmetry, and aesthetics that showed his potential. It wasn't long before he started to get a following. People realised that he had what it took to compete at a higher level. People encouraged Dauda to focus on national competitions, where he would face the top bodybuilders in the country.

SAMSON DAUDA

Dauda was very excited to be on the national stage. Only the most disciplined and dedicated athletes emerge victorious in these competitions, showcasing their best talent. It was hard work preparing for his first national competition. Dauda knew he needed to work hard and get better so he could compete well in the UK. This required modifying his diet, refining his workout routines, and ensuring he worked every muscle group to its maximum capacity. When Dauda became a national hero, he had an immediate impact. He brought a physique that combined mass and symmetry, a difficult balance in the sport of bodybuilding. His stage presence was strong, and his posing routine showed that he knew how to show off his strengths and minimise his weaknesses. Dauda's ability to show his physique in the best possible light is a skill that separates competent bodybuilders from great ones. Dauda worked hard to win the competition. He made a strong impression on the judges and got recognition for his overall development and presentation. Competing on the national stage not only raised Dauda's profile but also showed how hard he had worked. He was a national competitor with serious

SAMSON DAUDA

potential. Dauda's success on the national stage also changed how he approached sports. To do well at this level, he had to plan ahead and take care of himself throughout the year. National events require high conditioning and precise timing. Dauda had to learn how to build muscle in the off-season while getting lean and ready for competitions. Dauda approached this task with the same discipline and focus that had gotten him to this point. It was about showing himself and others that he could compete with the best. His performance in national competitions attracted a lot of attention from people in the business, sponsors, and other athletes. This exposure helped Dauda get the resources and support he needed to keep improving and reach bigger goals. Samson Dauda's entry onto the national stage was a big moment for his bodybuilding career. It was the result of years of hard work and dedication and also the beginning of his success in the sport. Dauda's ability to perform at a high level in these competitions showed that he had the potential to go even further, setting up his future success on the international bodybuilding scene.

SAMSON DAUDA

Rising in the Rankings

Samson Dauda's climb to the top of the bodybuilding rankings has been steady and focused. Perseverance, discipline, and a relentless pursuit of excellence characterise Dauda's journey. He rose in the rankings slowly, learning from setbacks and making adjustments to stand out in a tough field. Dauda learned bodybuilding early on, which helped him become successful later on. He became known for his size, symmetry, and stage presence. But he knew he needed to do more to be successful at both the national and international levels. Dauda had to work hard to improve his bodybuilding skills by training, eating healthy, looking good, and presenting himself. Dauda's rise was largely due to his dedication to getting in shape. Dauda knew that building muscle was not enough. He needed to be a well-rounded individual, combining both strength and beauty. This meant making sure his body was balanced and symmetrical, so his muscles worked together and no part was too big or too small. Dauda worked hard to get the right body weight, which helped him become popular

SAMSON DAUDA

with judges and fans. Dauda became more competitive, but he also saw these competitions as chances to test himself against the best. Dauda learned from each competition and made adjustments to improve. Dauda became very popular because he kept getting better after each competition. Dauda used feedback from judges and fellow competitors to fine-tune his physique. He started competing at higher-profile events, like the Arnold Classic and other major bodybuilding competitions. These competitions attract some of the best bodybuilders in the world, and placing well at these events shows how talented an athlete is at the sport. Dauda started to climb in the rankings after these events. His size, symmetry, and conditioning helped him stand out, and he always brought an improved version of himself to each competition. Dauda became a professional bodybuilder when he earned his pro card. This achievement not only raised his status but also allowed him to compete in more prestigious events. When a bodybuilder gets a pro card, it means they can compete with the best in the world. This was a big step for Dauda to move up in the rankings and show what he can do internationally. As Dauda got better, people noticed him not only for his body but also for being consistent. Dauda embraced this challenge to stay at the top of bodybuilding. He became known for his ability to bring a better package each time he took the stage. Dauda placed well in several high-profile competitions, making him one of the sport's rising stars. Dauda got higher in the rankings because of how he thinks about playing soccer. Dauda has been successful because he is mentally tough and determined. Dauda has been able to keep climbing the ranks even when faced with challenges. Samson Dauda's rise in the bodybuilding rankings is a testimony to his work ethic, discipline, and passion for the sport. His ability to improve with each competition, his focus on having a well-rounded body, and his mental toughness have all helped him climb. Dauda persists in competing at the highest levels and remains a formidable presence.

Gaining Recognition in the Bodybuilding Community

SAMSON DAUDA

Samson Dauda's journey to becoming known in the bodybuilding community is a story of perseverance, refinement, and a relentless drive to stand out in a very competitive sport. Dauda was born in Nigeria and moved to the United Kingdom. Once he established himself, his clear goal was to become one of the best. This journey was about earning the respect and attention of a community that is known for its high standards and critical eye for detail. Dauda's introduction to bodybuilding was somewhat unconventional. He didn't want to become a bodybuilder when he was young. He tried different sports when he was younger, but eventually he liked weightlifting and getting fit. Dauda started bodybuilding as a way to stay fit. His natural size and genetic predisposition to muscle growth made him stand out early on, but he quickly realised that raw talent alone would not be enough to get recognition in the community. Dauda started his bodybuilding career by participating in local competitions. These local contests greatly enhanced Dauda's understanding of the sport. He learned that bodybuilding was not just about who could put on the most muscle but who could present the best

SAMSON DAUDA

overall package. Because he knew he needed to do more to enter the bodybuilding ranks, Dauda focused on these aspects. Dauda became famous when he started doing well in local contests. His performances started to get the attention of fans and competitors alike. Dauda had a body that stood out. He had broad shoulders, a thick chest, and well-developed legs. But people were impressed by his ability to control his body on stage, not just how big he was. Dauda quickly learned how to pose, knowing that the way a bodybuilder looks can be just as important as the muscle itself. This careful attention helped him stand out from other talented competitors. As Dauda continued to improve and compete, he started to get more attention from the bodybuilding community.

Social media was important in this stage of his career because it allowed him to share his progress with a bigger audience. Dauda's constant posting of his training, diet, and competition prep helped him build a dedicated following. Many fans liked his honesty and work ethic. Dauda became famous when he started competing in national and international competitions. Dauda had to

SAMSON DAUDA

improve his game to compete against some of the best bodybuilders in the world. The bodybuilding community is quick to recognize outstanding athletes, but they also dismiss those who don't perform well. Dauda understood this and worked hard to make sure that his physique could compete at the highest levels. Dauda's journey started when he earned his pro card. This achievement allowed Dauda to compete in bigger and more important events, where the best people in the world competed for recognition. Dauda became famous here because he had a lovely body that impressed both fans and judges. His performances at high-profile competitions like the Arnold Classic helped him become a rising star in the sport. Another important part of Dauda's rise in the bodybuilding community was his ability to keep improving. Bodybuilding is a sport where progress is everything and stagnation can be the death of a career. Dauda worked hard to get stronger, fitter, and better on stage. This helped him win many competitions. He was able to come back stronger and better each time he competed, which was important in getting the respect of his peers and the bodybuilding community at large.

SAMSON DAUDA

Dauda's rise to prominence in the bodybuilding community was not just about winning competitions. It was also about his professionalism, work ethic, and ability to connect with fans. His respect extended beyond his physical appearance. His journey shows that in bodybuilding, recognition comes not only from building a good body but also from building a reputation as a dedicated and passionate athlete who is always trying to improve. As Dauda's profile got bigger, so did the opportunities. He began to get sponsorships, appearances in the media, and invitations to even more prestigious competitions. He became a formidable force in the sport as his name began to spread internationally.

SAMSON DAUDA

CHAPTER 4: Building a Championship Physique

Building a championship body takes years of dedication, discipline, and a deep understanding of the human body. Samson Dauda has worked hard to build a body that looks appealing and can compete in professional bodybuilding. Dauda's commitment to building a championship physique has been the foundation of his success. He has always pushed the boundaries of what is possible in terms of size, symmetry, and conditioning. Dauda knew that he needed more than just strength or size to stand out in the highly competitive world of bodybuilding. Bodybuilding judges look for a complete package that includes not only muscle mass but also symmetry, proportion, conditioning, and presentation. Dauda has spent years fine-tuning his training, diet, and lifestyle. Dauda's approach to training is one of the main reasons he has built a championship physique. Bodybuilding requires a combination of heavy lifting to build muscle and a variety of exercises to ensure balance

SAMSON DAUDA

and symmetry. Dauda's training regimen caters to both these aspects. Dauda ensures that every muscle group receives attention in his workouts. This way of doing things helps him avoid making some muscles bigger than others, which can make a bodybuilder look bad. Dauda uses a lot of different training techniques to build muscle density and definition. Techniques like supersets, drop sets, and time under tension make his workouts harder and make muscles grow faster. Dauda employs these techniques to challenge his muscles, compelling them to adjust and expand. Building the kind of muscles required to compete at the highest levels of bodybuilding requires this level of intensity. Another important part of Daus training is his focus on form and technique. Dauda knows it's important to lift heavy weights correctly to grow muscles and avoid injury. Dauda makes sure that he is targeting the correct muscles during each exercise, which makes for more effective workouts. Dauda can build a big, balanced body. Building a strong body is not just about going to the gym. Food is just as important in this process. Dauda designs his diet to provide his body with the necessary nutrients to build muscle, recover

SAMSON DAUDA

from intense workouts, and maintain a low body fat percentage. His nutrition plan is high in protein, which is important for muscle repair and growth, but also includes the right balance of carbohydrates and fats to fuel his workouts and support overall health. Dauda's approach to nutrition is very focused. He follows a strict plan for eating that makes sure he eats the right foods at the right times. This level of discipline is important for any bodybuilder who wants to build a championship physique. Even small changes in diet can have a big impact on a bodybuilder's progress.

In the weeks leading up to a competition, Dauda's diet gets even more precise as he works to get in shape. This entails monitoring his macronutrient intake and making necessary adjustments to ensure his muscles are full and well-defined, while simultaneously minimising his body fat. Success for Dauda involves training, eating well, and recovering from injuries. A championship physique is a lot of work, and without proper recovery, it's impossible to make progress. Dauda makes sure that he gets enough sleep each night to repair his muscles and grow. He uses

SAMSON DAUDA

stretching, massage, and sometimes cryotherapy to make muscles less sore and improve blood flow. These recovery strategies help Dauda train harder while reducing the risk of injury. Dauda pays close attention to details when it comes to bodybuilding. The process of building a championship physique requires both physical strength and mental toughness. Dauda's discipline and focus are crucial for adhering to a training plan and maintaining a healthy diet. Dauda's ability to stay motivated and push through challenges has been a key factor in his success. He approaches each workout, meal, and recovery session like a champion, understanding that every detail matters when it comes to building a winning physique. As Dauda's career has progressed, he has always worked on building a championship physique. Each competition gives him valuable feedback, which he can use to improve his training, nutrition, and presentation. Dauda's willingness to change and improve has been one of the reasons she has risen in the bodybuilding world. He knows that bodybuilding is a constantly changing sport, so he is always looking for ways to improve his physique. Samson Dauda's journey to building a championship physique is a testament to his work ethic, discipline, and deep understanding of the sport. He trains hard, eats well, and rests well. He also keeps his mind strong so he can compete well. Dauda has become renowned as a top bodybuilder by constantly improving his techniques and striving for perfection.

Perfecting Muscle Mass and Symmetry

Samson Dauda is very good at bodybuilding because he can make his muscles big and straight, which are very important in the sport. Dauda has always tried to build a body that is balanced and looks good. This is a combination of power and proportion that sets him apart from many other bodybuilders. To do this, you need to train well, eat well, and be aware of your body. Dauda has mastered these things over time. Dauda knew that building muscle mass alone wasn't enough to succeed at the highest levels of the sport. Size is important, but bodybuilding also involves the distribution of mass throughout the body. Judges evaluate competitors based on the size and coordination of their muscles. Dauda has

SAMSON DAUDA

spent years working on his physique to achieve this balance. Dauda's physique is unique in that he can carry a lot of muscle without losing symmetry. Dauda's impressively developed broad shoulders, thick chest, and powerful legs are what set his physique apart. In bodybuilding, balance is important. If a bodybuilder has a big upper body but not enough legs, judges will say they are not adequate enough. Dauda exercises every muscle group equally intensely, ensuring he doesn't neglect any part of his body. Dauda follows a specific training plan to achieve a balanced body. His workouts focus on each muscle group carefully and emphasise its size and shape. Dauda lifts a lot to gain weight, but he also exercises to make his body look symmetrical. He uses a combination of mass-building and sculpting exercises to add muscle without losing the aesthetic appeal that is important in bodybuilding. Dauda focuses on weak points when trying to build muscles and look symmetrical. Dauda has shown a keen ability to identify and address areas of their physique that develop more slowly than others. By focusing on his weak points, he has been able to build up muscle groups and create a

SAMSON DAUDA

body that is as close to perfect as possible. Dauda's constant self-assessment and willingness to improve have helped her rise through the ranks of the bodybuilding world. Nutrition also helps Dauda build muscle mass while keeping her body symmetrical.

To build muscles and recover, you need a healthy mix of protein, carbs, and fat. Dauda carefully plans his diet to ensure he gets the right amount of nutrients to build muscle without adding too much body fat. This balance is especially important as he approaches competitions, when peak conditioning becomes important. Dauda is able to show his size and symmetry by keeping his body fat low while still supporting muscle growth. One of the challenges of building both muscle mass and symmetry is making sure that the body grows in proportion as it adds size. This requires a deep understanding of how different muscle groups work together and how to train them in a way that encourages balanced growth. The Dauda training approach reflects this understanding. He watches how his muscles respond to different exercises and adjusts them if needed to make sure he's working in

SAMSON DAUDA

the right places. He may change his training to focus more on his legs if he feels that his upper body is growing faster. This awareness helps him keep his body symmetrical even as he gains muscle mass. Dauda's mastery of posing has also been crucial in showing off his muscle mass and symmetry. Posing is a form of bodybuilding that allows competitors to show off their bodies in the best way possible. Dauda has spent a long time perfecting how he poses. This helps him show off his positive qualities and hide his negative ones. His ability to present his body in a way that shows both size and balance has been a key part of his success on stage. Samson Dauda's focus on muscle mass and symmetry has been the foundation of his rise in bodybuilding. He trains hard, eats well, and looks good. This helps him have a strong and attractive body. Dauda's commitment to both size and proportion is what makes him one of the best bodybuilders in the world. His unwavering commitment to these principles has enabled him to enhance his skills and push the boundaries of the sport, establishing him as a formidable competitor.

SAMSON DAUDA

Tailoring His Diet for Maximum Growth

Samson Dauda's success in bodybuilding is not only a result of his dedication to training but also of his careful attention to nutrition. Choosing the right food for him has been crucial in his journey. This has helped him gain the weight, strength, and symmetry that he needs to compete well. Dauda believes that food is more than just fuel. It's a tool to help muscles grow, recover, and perform better overall. In the world of bodybuilding, diet is very important. A healthy diet helps athletes gain muscle and keep their body fat low, so they look healthy on stage. Dauda's approach to his diet reflects the discipline and precision needed to reach this balance. Dauda plans and times every meal to meet his body's needs. Dauda eats mainly protein, the building block of muscle. Protein is important for making muscles stronger and bigger, especially after intense workouts. Dauda eats lots of nutritious protein like chicken, turkey, lean beef, eggs, and fish. These sources provide him with the amino acids he needs to grow and recover. Dauda adjusts his protein intake daily, usually consuming between 1.2

SAMSON DAUDA

and 1.5 grams of protein per pound of body weight. This amount of protein helps him keep muscle and lose fat. Dauda eats mainly carbohydrates. Carbohydrates give him the energy he needs to train hard and push his body. However, not all carbohydrates are the same. Dauda focuses on complex carbohydrates like sweet potatoes, brown rice, oats, and whole grains, which give him a steady release of energy and help him stay in shape. These slow-digesting carbs help him stay healthy during training. Dauda's diet is also timed well. He eats most of his carbs before and after working out. Pre-workout carbs give him the energy he needs to perform at his best, while post-workout carbs help him recover. Dauda makes sure that his body is always ready to grow and recover. Fats are another key component of Dauda's diet. Avocados, nuts, seeds, and olive oil provide essential fatty acids that help hormone production, especially testosterone, which is important for muscle growth. These fats also help keep joints healthy, which is especially important for someone like Dauda who regularly works out hard. Dauda eats healthy fats to stay healthy and perform well. Daudas diet is also about balance and consistency. He eats five to six meals a day and breaks them up every few hours to keep his body in an anabolic state. By eating healthy food regularly, his muscles get the protein and carbs they need to grow. It also helps keep his blood sugar levels stable and gives him energy throughout the day.

Dauda significantly increases his caloric intake during the off-season when he concentrates on building muscle mass. Dauda eats more calories than his body needs to maintain his weight. By doing this, he creates the ideal environment for muscle growth by having an excess of nutrients that help build new muscle tissue. However, Dauda makes sure that this surplus comes from clean, whole foods instead of processed or unhealthy options. This method helps him gain weight without adding too much fat, keeping his body lean even when he's bulking up. When Dauda is preparing for competitions, his focus shifts to reducing body fat while keeping as much muscle mass as possible. This phase forces his body to burn fat for energy. Dauda becomes even more careful with his diet, tracking every calorie and macronutrient to

SAMSON DAUDA

make sure he is losing fat while keeping muscle. During this phase, his protein intake increases to help preserve muscle tissue, and his carbohydrate and fat intake decreases to help lose weight. Dauda's diet also depends on water. Water is essential for muscles, digestion, and overall health. Dauda drinks plenty of water throughout the day to help his body's metabolic processes and prevent dehydration. Hydration also helps Dauda stay full, which is important for getting the look she wants on stage. Samson Dauda knows how food affects muscle growth and how well he can perform. He is a talented bodybuilder because he gives his body the right nutrients at the right time. He looks great because he works hard in and out of the gym.

Intense Workout Regimens and Recovery Techniques

Samson Dauda, a professional bodybuilder, has made a name for himself in the competitive bodybuilding world with his intense workouts and disciplined recovery techniques. His journey to become one of the top

SAMSON DAUDA

bodybuilders requires a balance of physical exertion and strategic recovery. Dauda's training philosophy focuses on being precise and having a plan. He does specific workouts for different parts of the competition preparation. He trains five to six days a week, and each session targets specific muscle groups. Samson uses a combination of strength training, hypertrophy, and conditioning exercises to build a balanced and symmetrical physique. He tries to work multiple muscle groups each day to grow and shape his body in line with competitive requirements. Dauda focuses on doing rigorous exercises like squats, deadlifts, and bench presses when he trains. These exercises help him build strength and mass in multiple muscle groups at the same time. His workouts are usually high-volume and involve multiple sets and rep ranges that challenge his muscles to the point of fatigue. His leg days are usually very busy. He uses exercises like squats, leg presses, and lunges to work his lower body hard. He performs a variety of exercises to ensure he targets every muscle group. Samson Dauda uses isolation exercises as part of his workout plan. These exercises work on specific muscles,

SAMSON DAUDA

making it easier to build muscle definition. He ensures the completeness of his body by employing exercises such as bicep curls, lateral raises, and leg extensions. His body is well balanced because of his dedication to symmetry. Dauda strategically approaches cardio. Many people think that bodybuilders only focus on weightlifting, but cardiovascular fitness is important for keeping your body fat low, especially during competition prep. Dauda uses steady-state cardio or high-intensity interval training (HIIT) depending on where he is in his training. This balance ensures that he can keep muscle mass while losing excess fat. Training intensity alone is not enough to meet the demands of professional bodybuilding. Samson Dauda's overall success depends on his recovery. His approach to recovery is multifaceted and carefully planned so that his body can handle the intensity of his workouts. Dauda's recovery plan includes nutrition. He eats a high-calorie diet of protein, healthy fats, and complex carbs to repair muscles and replenish energy. It's important for him to eat quickly after working out to recover.

SAMSON DAUDA

Protein shakes with amino acids help muscles heal faster after intense workouts. Sleep is another important component of recovery. Samson knows that the body repairs and grows during rest. He wants to get at least 7 to 9 hours of quality sleep every night. This practice not only helps him build muscle, but it also helps him stay focused and ready for his next training session. Dauda incorporates active recovery techniques in his routine. Especially when he lifts a lot of weight and trains frequently, it's crucial to stretch and move around to prevent injuries and maintain flexibility. Foam rolling and deep tissue massages help relax muscles, promote better blood circulation, and reduce soreness. Moving around helps him recover faster between workouts, so his muscles stay flexible and less likely to hurt. Samson also turns to more advanced recovery methods, like cryotherapy and infrared sauna treatments. Cryotherapy, which involves exposing the body to frigid temperatures, helps reduce inflammation and speed up muscle recovery. Infrared saunas promote relaxation and detoxification, improving circulation. These treatments make Dauda stronger and better able to handle more

SAMSON DAUDA

physical challenges. In the weeks before competitions, Samson's ways of recovering are even more important. His body experiences significant physical stress as he reduces body fat and intensifies his workouts. To manage fatigue and prevent burnout, Dauda takes extra measures, such as lowering the weight or volume of his lifts, to aid in muscle recovery while still exercising. Samson Dauda trains hard and recovers quickly, which helps him stay stronger. He has developed strength, resilience, and mental toughness by focusing on both physical and mental aspects of bodybuilding.

The Role of Supplementation in His Success

Samson Dauda, a professional bodybuilder, knows how important it is to take supplements to reach his goals. Supplementation is key to improving his performance, recovery, and overall progress. Dauda, who competes at the highest level, uses supplements to help him train better and get the results he needs in bodybuilding. Dauda heavily incorporates protein supplements into her diet. He trains a lot and needs protein to repair and grow his muscles. Dauda eats a lot of chicken, fish, and eggs, but it's challenging to get enough protein from whole foods alone. Protein powders, especially whey and casein, help him get the protein he needs without making his stomach too full. Dauda eats whey protein right after his workout. This helps his muscles get the amino acids they need to recover and grow quickly, reducing the chance of them breaking down. Dauda might take Casein before bed to give his muscles a steady stream of amino acids. Dauda supplements with BCAAs. Leucine, isoleucine, and valine are essential amino acids that help muscles recover and reduce exercise-induced fatigue. Dauda uses BCAAs during his workouts to keep energy up and reduce muscle soreness. He also uses essential amino acids (EAAs) to help muscle protein synthesis and recovery. These supplements are especially helpful when Dauda is cutting weight for a competition or when he is training hard. Creatine monohydrate is another supplement that is important for Dauda's success. Studies have demonstrated that Creatine enhances strength, power, and muscle mass. Creatine helps make more ATP (adenosine triphosphate), which is the main

SAMSON DAUDA

energy source for heavy lifting. For someone like Dauda, who is always pushing his body to lift heavier weights and perform at its best, creatine helps him stay strong during his training sessions. This supplement helps him keep getting better and stronger, so he can compete in bodybuilding. Dauda takes pre-workout supplements.

These formulas often contain ingredients like caffeine, beta-alanine, and nitric oxide boosters that give you an energy boost, improve focus, and improve blood flow to the muscles. These supplements help Dauda keep his workouts intense and mentally sharp. Caffeine is crucial in this situation because it makes you feel alert and also helps burn fat. This is crucial when you're preparing for a competition and striving to lose weight. Dauda supplements his recovery and helps him perform better. He uses glutamine, which helps his muscles recover, immune system, and gut health, often after intense workouts. After his workouts, glutamine helps his muscles heal faster and feel less sore. This lets Dauda train hard all the time without getting tired or overtraining. Electrolyte supplements also aid in Dauda's

SAMSON DAUDA

recovery. A proper balance of sodium, potassium, magnesium, and calcium is important to prevent cramps, dehydration, and fatigue. Samson uses electrolyte powder or drinks to stay hydrated and work well during his workouts and between them. Dauda also makes multivitamins and mineral supplements. Even though his diet is full of nutrient-dense foods, it's not always possible to get all the body needs through food alone. Multivitamins help his body get the vitamins and minerals it needs, like vitamin D, magnesium, and zinc. These vitamins and minerals are important for health, bone strength, and muscle function. Dauda takes fish oil and omega-3 supplements to keep her joints healthy and reduce inflammation. Because he lifts a lot and trains hard, it's essential for his joints to be healthy. Omega-3 fatty acids shield his joints from damage, enabling him to maintain his high-level training without risk of injury. Samson Dauda takes supplements to help his body work harder. Samson Dauda uses these supplements to optimise every aspect of his training and recovery for success.

SAMSON DAUDA

CHAPTER 5: Mindset of a Champion

Samson Dauda is proficient at bodybuilding because he is strong mentally and stays focused. A champion's mindset helps him overcome difficulties, stay focused, and stay true to his goals. Dauda's mental fortitude is what drives him in every aspect of his career, from his rigorous workout routines to the sacrifices he makes in his personal life. Dauda is known for his discipline. Dauda knows that to be successful in bodybuilding, you have to work hard every day for a long time. Dauda follows a strict diet, exercises, and recovery plan with a sense of duty and purpose. He stays on schedule and follows his diet. He knows that every little thing he does helps him succeed. This practice goes beyond the gym and kitchen. Dauda knows that how he feels mentally affects how he approaches each day. He is known for staying focused despite distractions. Dauda has a mental resilience that allows him to block out negativity and stay focused on what needs done. He is very focused, which makes him different from other competitors. He trains his mind to deal with the challenges of being an

SAMSON DAUDA

elite athlete. Dauda's champion mindset plays a crucial role in his ability to maintain patience and trust in the process. Bodybuilding results don't come overnight. The results of months, if not years, of hard work are muscle growth, fat loss, and physical transformation. Many people find this delayed gratification frustrating, leading to doubt and, in some cases, quitting altogether. Dauda embraces the long journey. He knows that being successful in bodybuilding is about more than just getting there. He gets excited about making small improvements, doing more exercises, and making progress. He stays focused on his goals because he knows that all his hard work will lead to the body he wants. Dauda also believes in self-discipline when it comes to controlling his emotions and keeping a positive attitude. In bodybuilding, mental and emotional stress can have a big effect on performance, from physical fatigue to self-doubt. Dauda says that being emotionally stable is important for staying on track. He says that it's important to have a supportive environment where he can channel positive energy and keep negative influences at bay.

SAMSON DAUDA

Dauda is calm and composed when faced with setbacks, whether it's an injury or a poor performance. He can control his emotions and overcome problems quickly. He focuses on long-term goals instead of short-term disappointments. Dauda has developed a strong sense of mental toughness over the years. This toughness is what allows him to push past mental barriers that often come up during intense training sessions. When a person feels worn out and wonders if they can do more, they use their mental strength to get through. Dauda is an athlete who embraces discomfort and pushes his limits. He sees these moments of challenge as opportunities to test his mental and physical limits and knows that they are steps toward greatness. Dauda thinks it's important to have a positive attitude about both success and failure. He knows not every competition or training session will go well. Dauda uses these moments as motivation to improve. He sees failure as an opportunity to improve and move forward. This mindset helps him keep learning and using his mistakes to push harder in the future. In many ways, his career is defined by his resilience in the face of adversity. It's not about failing, but about not giving up. Samson Dauda is always willing to learn and change. He knows that bodybuilding is a constantly changing sport, and staying ahead requires both physical work and mental agility. Dauda is open to learning new ways to train, eat better, and recover faster. He approaches every aspect of training with a sense of curiosity and a desire to improve himself. This growth mindset allows him to keep improving his approach and never get complacent. Samson Dauda believes that being a champion is more than just physical strength. It's about mental strength, discipline, patience, and a never-ending pursuit of excellence. His success in bodybuilding shows how powerful the mind can be and how it can shape a career.

Mental Toughness in the Face of Challenges

Samson Dauda's rise in the bodybuilding world has not been without its challenges, and his mental toughness has been key to overcoming them. Dauda has had to overcome many obstacles as a professional athlete in a highly competitive sport. But his ability to stay mentally

SAMSON DAUDA

strong in the face of adversity has been one of the things that sets him apart. Dauda's mental toughness begins with an unwavering determination to succeed, regardless of the challenges he faces. In bodybuilding, the path to success is long and tough, filled with periods of self-doubt, physical fatigue, and gruelling competition preparations. Bodybuilding requires patience and a firm belief in the process. Samson Dauda gets it. He knows that growth takes time, and this awareness has helped him develop a mindset that embraces the grind. Dauda knows that there is no shortcut to success, and he has developed the resilience to push through the toughest times when results are slow to come. Dauda has had to deal with a lot of pressure to keep improving. As a bodybuilder, keeping things the same is never enough. He needs to keep pushing his limits, whether it's lifting heavier weights, improving his physique, or perfecting his diet. To keep improving, you need a special kind of mental toughness. It's not just about physical endurance; it's also about having the mental clarity to set realistic goals, the patience to reach them, and the strength to keep moving forward even when progress is slow. Dauda

SAMSON DAUDA

accepts the challenge and knows that real progress often happens in small, almost invisible steps. Instead of being frustrated by slow progress, he uses it as motivation, knowing that every step forward brings him closer to his ultimate goal. Every professional athlete has to deal with injuries, and Dauda is no exception. A bodybuilder's injuries can inflict physical and mental harm. The road to recovery can be long and uncertain, filled with moments of frustration and fear. But Dauda has shown remarkable mental toughness when it comes to dealing with injuries. Instead of letting them ruin his training and motivation, he uses them to change how he approaches things, focus on getting better, and come back stronger. This ability to stay positive and determined in the face of physical setbacks is a sign of his resilience. Dauda has been able to keep his mental focus by seeing injuries as temporary obstacles instead of permanent roadblocks. This has been important for his long-term success. Dauda is mentally strong and can handle the stress of competition. Bodybuilding requires a lot of physical and mental strength. Judges' scrutiny, fans' expectations, and the

SAMSON DAUDA

pressure to perform at the highest level can be overwhelming.

Dauda's ability to stay calm and keep his confidence has been important to his success. He has learned to trust his preparation, knowing that his months of work will pay off. Dauda maintains his mental sharpness and prevents external pressures from distracting him by concentrating on his controllable aspects of competition, such as his presentation and posing. Dauda's mental toughness includes his ability to handle failure. In bodybuilding, like in any other sport, losses are inevitable. There will always be competitions where things don't go as planned and the result falls short of expectations. Dauda sees these moments of failure as opportunities to learn and grow. He has a mindset that sees failure as part of the process. Rather than succumbing to discouragement, Dauda scrutinises his performances and pinpoints areas for improvement. He is able to turn failure into fuel for future success. It allows him to move forward with renewed energy, knowing that each setback is a step toward greater success. Dauda knows that self-belief is important for building mental toughness. In a sport where everyone is trying to be the best, confidence is important. When external validation doesn't come, self-belief becomes even more important. Dauda has cultivated an inner confidence that keeps him grounded even when others doubt him. This feeling of self-assurance makes him want to keep going, work harder, and try harder, even when things get tough. Samson Dauda is a professional bodybuilder because he is mentally tough. He has been successful because he is strong, determined, and believes in himself. Dauda demonstrated that mental strength is mental as well as physical.

Staying Focused on Long-Term Goals

Samson Dauda's journey in bodybuilding shows what it means to focus on long-term goals. Dauda's ability to keep his eyes on the big picture has been a key part of his success. Dedication, patience, and a deep understanding that greatness doesn't happen overnight have built his career. Dauda sets his long-term goals by

SAMSON DAUDA

having a clear idea of where he wants to go. Starting his career, he wanted to be a top bodybuilder. This meant more than just competing; it meant constantly improving his physique and performance over time. This kind of thinking requires the ability to set smaller, more manageable goals that match the ultimate goal. Dauda doesn't just focus on winning the next competition; she focuses on building a body that can compete at the highest level for years to come. Dauda's ability to stay focused on long-term goals is key to staying focused. His training schedule, diet, and recovery protocols all match his bigger goals. Bodybuilding is a sport that requires a lot of hard work every day. A single workout or a week of training won't make much difference in the long run. Dauda's success comes from showing up every day, doing his work, and following his plan. He knows that each meal, rep, and recovery session is a part of his future success. Dauda is better at managing his career when things go wrong. Setbacks, such as an injury, a poor competition result, or a plateau in physical progress, can easily discourage us. Dauda sees these challenges as temporary. He never lets a negative day or

SAMSON DAUDA

season distract him from his goals. Instead, he thinks about the bigger picture and realises that failures are part of the process and can help him get better. His ability to stay calm and keep things in perspective is a hallmark of his mental strength. Dauda believes that to be successful in bodybuilding for a long time, you need to keep learning and changing. The sport is always changing, and there are always new ways to train, eat healthy, and recover. Instead of being complacent or sticking to one method, Dauda embraces the need for growth. He's always looking for ways to improve his approach, whether that's trying new exercises, changing his diet, or adding new recovery techniques. He is always willing to change, even if it's small and slow. Dauda plans his training and competitions carefully to reach his long-term goals. Bodybuilding is not a sport where athletes can be in peak condition all year long. Dauda knows it's important to plan his training and competition schedule so he can do his best when it matters most. This means understanding his body and how it responds to different training phases. Dauda consistently concentrates on his objective of enhancing his body's

SAMSON DAUDA

performance. Quick results or the urge to rush things along don't distract him. Instead, he believes in his plan and waits patiently because real progress takes time. Dauda can focus on long-term goals because he has a strong mind. Bodybuilding is as much a mental as it is a physical challenge. The constant pressure to improve can wear down even the strongest athletes. But Dauda's mental toughness keeps him focused, even when the road gets tough. He has made ways to deal with doubt and fatigue, like using visualisation techniques, meditation, or reminding himself why he started the journey in the first place. He stays motivated and focused even when things get tough. Samson Dauda is a top bodybuilder because of his long-term goals. His career shows how patience, discipline, and the ability to keep moving forward can make a big difference. Dauda has set himself apart in a sport where many athletes struggle to stay focused over the long haul. His journey is a reminder that success in bodybuilding and life is not about quick wins.

Dealing with Competition Pressure

SAMSON DAUDA

Samson Dauda's success in bodybuilding is because he can handle the pressure of competition. It's crucial for athletes to prepare both mentally and physically in a sport that judges everything from muscle strength to training efficiency and appearance. Dauda has come up with ways to handle the stress of performing in front of judges and fans. Dauda handles competition pressure by preparing meticulously. He believes that confidence comes from knowing you've done everything you can to be ready for the moment. This means training hard, eating well, and looking appealing in pictures. Dauda prepares for competition by preparing everything ahead of time. He knows that if he steps on stage, he has already worked hard. This preparedness allows him to focus on the task at hand instead of getting overwhelmed by nerves or second-guessing his efforts. Dauda also says that mental preparation and visualisation are important for dealing with competition pressure. Before he competes, he spends time thinking about how he will perform on stage. This mental rehearsal not only acclimates Dauda to the environment but also instil a sense of control in her. By visualising success, he

SAMSON DAUDA

prepares his mind to handle the real-life situation with the same level of poise and calm. Dauda's ability to remain present in the moment is a crucial aspect of his approach to competitive pressure. It's simple to get caught up in thoughts about whether he'll win, how the judges will score him, or how he compares to the other competitors. But Dauda has learned to focus on what he can do right now. He can stay focused and prevent thoughts of victory or defeat from distracting him by focusing on his breathing, posture, and posing routine. He stays calm and can do his job well. Dauda needs to control his emotions when he competes, both on and off the stage. When you try hard and don't get what you want, you might feel anxious, stressed, or frustrated.

Dauda has learned how to handle emotions that come up when people compete. Dauda manages his emotions through meditation, deep breathing, and talking to his support team. Dauda's support system helps him cope with the pressure of competition. Having a strong team behind him is both emotional and practical support. His coach helps Dauda train and prepare for competition.

SAMSON DAUDA

The emotional support from friends and family helps keep him grounded and reminds him of the bigger picture. Dauda can focus on what he needs to do knowing that he has people around him who believe in his abilities. Dauda also approaches competition with a mindset of growth instead of perfection. He knows that he can't control everything on competition day, even if he works hard. The sport is unpredictable due to judges' decisions, competitors' performance, and even minor pose mistakes. Dauda sees every competition as an opportunity to learn and grow. This way of thinking helps relieve stress by focusing on improving rather than achieving perfection. Even when the results aren't what he wanted, Dauda uses them to motivate him to improve. Dauda has learned to see competition as a privilege, not a burden. He competes at a high level because of the hard work and dedication he has put into the sport. Dauda thinks that bodybuilding is exciting because of the pressure. It inspires him to push himself beyond his limits, challenge his mind and body, and strive for excellence. Dauda has turned pressure into a source of energy. Samson Dauda's approach to dealing with

SAMSON DAUDA

competition pressure is a combination of mental preparation, emotional management, and a deep belief in his abilities. His ability to stay calm, focused, and resilient in the face of pressure is a testament to his mental toughness and his years of experience in the sport. Dauda has mastered the art of performing under pressure.

Visualising Success: Samson's Mental Strategies

Samson Dauda is a bodybuilder who works hard and uses visualisation to achieve success. Many elite athletes use visualisation as a technique to stay focused, confident, and prepared for competition. This mental practice is as important to his success as his time at the gym. Dauda starts by seeing the end goal clearly in his mind. Dauda imagines himself winning a competition or achieving a long-term goal. This practice is about getting his mind ready for the process of getting there. In his visualisations, Dauda walks through every stage of competition: the moment he steps on stage, how he

SAMSON DAUDA

presents himself to the judges, and how he performs each pose with precision and confidence. This mental rehearsal helps reduce anxiety by making the event feel familiar before he even gets to it. Dauda has already experienced the competition many times before, so he can approach it calmly and confidently. Dauda says that visualisation helps him stay focused. Bodybuilding requires a lot of focus, both for doing physical tasks and for keeping your mind clear during long training sessions and competitions. Dauda keeps his mind sharp and focused by visualising his goals often. When distractions or doubts might come up, Dauda goes back to the mental images he has made and reminds himself of his ultimate goal. Small problems or external pressures cannot distract him with this focus. Dauda uses visualisation to make himself more confident. Competing at the highest level of bodybuilding comes with a lot of pressure, and confidence is important for how well an athlete does. For Dauda, seeing himself succeed in his mind helps him feel positive about himself.

SAMSON DAUDA

He doesn't just think about what will happen; he also thinks about how he will handle obstacles along the way, like being tired from training, being watched by judges, or having a tough competition. This helps him prepare mentally for situations that might surprise him in real life. Instead, Dauda can approach them with the knowledge that he has already overcome them mentally, which makes him better at performing under pressure. Dauda uses visualisation to see where he can improve. He thinks about what could go wrong and how he would react. Dauda imagines how he would respond if a pose didn't go as planned or he felt tired. This mental flexibility helps him adapt to competitions, where the unexpected can and often does happen. By mentally preparing for these moments, Dauda makes sure that he won't be surprised by small mistakes or unexpected difficulties. Dauda uses positive thinking and self-talk to improve his thinking and visualisation skills. Dauda also uses affirmations to remind him of his abilities. Dauda overcomes self-doubt by thinking positive, empowering thoughts. Positive self-talk improves his mood and strengthens the visualisations he already practises.

SAMSON DAUDA

Dauda creates a feedback loop that strengthens his resolve and belief in his ability to succeed. The Dauda visualisation technique is not limited to competition day. He also uses mental imagery in his training. Dauda mentally rehearses what it will be like to stand on stage and show off his work. This connection between his daily efforts and his ultimate goal keeps him motivated and focused, even during the hardest parts of his training. Dauda keeps a sense of purpose and direction by linking his actions now to his future success. In the end, Samson Dauda uses visualisation and mental strategies to improve his bodybuilding skills. He has been successful because of his ability to mentally prepare for success, stay focused under pressure, and build confidence through visualisation. Dauda believes bodybuilding is as much mental as physical, and his mental practices have helped him succeed on the world stage.

SAMSON DAUDA

CHAPTER 6: Competing at the Elite Level

Samson Dauda's rise to the top of bodybuilding is a testament to his work ethic, strategic approach, and focus. To do well in bodybuilding, you need to be strong physically, mentally, and emotionally. Not everyone can do it. Dauda's entire life revolves around preparing to perform on the world's biggest stages, where the margin for error is slim and the expectations are huge. To compete well, you need to be very strong and fit. Dauda worked hard for many years to get the body she needs to compete well. He designs his workouts to precisely shape each muscle group, maintaining symmetry, proportion, and conditioning. In competitive bodybuilding, merely possessing large muscles is not enough. You also need to look attractive and balanced. Dauda's ability to fine-tune his physique comes from years of understanding how his body reacts to different training stimuli, nutrition plans, and recovery techniques. His approach is as scientific as it is physical, constantly improving his strategy to reach peak performance at the right time. The key to competing at the elite level is timing and speaking for competitions. Bodybuilders like Dauda need to make sure they train and eat well before the event in order to be in good shape. This means making sure that they are in the best shape possible when they step on stage. Dauda works hard in the gym and takes care of his food to achieve peak performance. Dauda calculates every calorie, macronutrient, and supplement to aid in muscle growth and fat loss. In the weeks before a competition, Dauda begins to lose weight while keeping as much muscle as possible.

This requires a delicate balance, as losing too much fat too quickly can lead to muscle loss, while not losing enough can result in a softer appearance on stage. Competing at the elite level takes a lot of mental preparation. Dauda has developed a mindset that helps him stay calm under pressure, block out distractions, and focus on his performance. Bodybuilding requires intense mental preparation. An athlete's mental health can be affected by weeks or months of dieting, training, and

SAMSON DAUDA

practice. Dauda solves problems by setting clear goals, picturing his success, and focusing on the bigger picture. He's mentally tough enough to deal with injuries, plateaus, or the stress of competition day. One of the biggest challenges of being a top-tier athlete is dealing with the expectations that come with it. Dauda has to live up to the expectations of fans, sponsors, and judges. The pressure to improve and stay at the top of the sport is huge. But Dauda stays grounded and focuses on what he can control: his preparation, his performance, and his mindset. He knows that while he can't control the outcome or the opinions of the judges, he can control the effort he puts in, and that's where he puts his energy. Another important part of winning at the highest level is looking good. The way athletes pose significantly influences their evaluation. Even if a competitor has a great physique, their ability to pose effectively could potentially lead to their overlooked status. Dauda works hard to make sure that every pose shows his strengths and minimises his weaknesses. Dauda can pose confidently on the competition stage because he has practised for a long time and knows how to show his

SAMSON DAUDA

body in the best way. Being at the top requires managing the pressures of being in front of many people. The bodybuilding community often criticises Dauda. Social media has made it harder for athletes to deal with the opinions and expectations of many people around the world. Dauda is a professional who uses social media to connect with his followers and stay focused on his goals. He knows it's important to make a name for yourself in the bodybuilding world, but he doesn't let it distract him from his main goal of doing well. Despite the competition, Dauda remains respectful in bodybuilding. In a sport where athletes constantly compare themselves, Dauda maintains a sense of camaraderie and respect for his teammates. He knows that everyone on stage has done hard work and sacrifice, and this makes them all feel connected. Dauda wants to win, but he also likes the process and the people he meets along the way. When you compete at the highest level, you need to balance your physical, mental, and emotional abilities to perform well on stage. Samson To succeed at this level, Dauda's bodybuilding experience shows you need more than muscle. You need to think about everything, from how

SAMSON DAUDA

you prepare to how you perform. Dauda has earned his place among the best by showing what it takes to compete at the highest level in bodybuilding.

Qualifying for International Competitions

Samson Dauda's journey to qualify for international bodybuilding competitions has been one of perseverance, discipline, and planning. To compete in important sports like Mr. Olympia and Arnold Classic, you need to work hard, do well in qualifying events, and always do well. Dauda has worked hard for years to reach international competitions. The process for qualifying for international competitions usually starts with participation in regional and national events. Bodybuilders use these shows to show off their bodies and get recognition. Dauda competes in smaller competitions to build his reputation and gain experience. It's important to do well at this level to get noticed by judges and other bodybuilders and to get invited to bigger events. Dauda focused on improving his posing, conditioning, and overall appearance in these early competitions. Invitations to higher-level competitions, such as pro-qualifying events, often require winning or placing well at these shows. To be a good bodybuilder, they need to become professionals. Usually, this means getting an IFBB Pro Card. The IFBB is the bodybuilding organisation that runs professional competitions like the Mr. Olympia. Dauda's journey to get his Pro Card was a pivotal moment in his career. It marked the transition from being an amateur competitor to becoming a professional athlete. To earn a Pro Card, bodybuilders usually win or place highly in national or international qualifying competitions. These events are very competitive, with athletes trying to get Pro Cards that let them compete on the global stage. After a bodybuilder gets a Pro Card, they can start competing in IFBB-approved pro shows. The IFBB hosts a series of professional competitions around the world where bodybuilders have the chance to earn points or qualify for major events like the Mr. Olympia. Different categories divide pro shows, requiring athletes to select competitions according to their strengths, preparation, and timing. Dauda believes that choosing the right competitions is part of his plan to reach the highest level. Competing too often or without enough preparation can lead to poor performances, while competing strategically can help athletes get the points or qualifications they need. The point system is another important part of getting into international competitions. The IFBB uses a points-based system to qualify athletes for events like the Mr. Olympia. The higher an athlete ranks in these shows, the more points they get. At the end of the qualification period, the athletes with the most points and winners of certain pro shows get spots in the prestigious competitions. For bodybuilders like Dauda, keeping track of their competition schedule and making sure they compete enough to get points while also giving their bodies time to recover and peak is very important. Timing is another important factor for getting into international competitions. For athletes like Dauda, it's essential to reach their peak at the right time. Peaking refers to the process of getting the body ready for competition day. This involves months of training, diet, and recovery to make sure that muscles are full, defined, and well-conditioned when it matters most. Competing too early or too late in the season can affect an athlete's ability to peak well. Dauda has mastered the art of timing his preparation so that he is at his best at the right competitions, maximising his chances of qualifying for international events. The final step in qualifying for international competitions is to get the judges' and bodybuilding community's attention. Even with the best preparation, success in bodybuilding competitions comes down to how well an athlete looks on stage. Judges look for athletes who have a favourable combination of muscle mass, symmetry, conditioning, and presentation. Dauda has become famous because he keeps getting stronger and better at posing and performing on stage. Competing at the international level takes a lot more than just looking good. Dauda says that qualifying for events like the Mr. Olympia is the result of careful planning, relentless work, and a deep understanding of the sport. His success on the international stage shows that he can handle the complicated process of getting his pro card, competing in the right shows, performing at the right time, and impressing judges and fans.

SAMSON DAUDA

The Experience of Competing on the Olympia Stage

For Samson Dauda, competing at Olympia is the pinnacle of his bodybuilding career. The Olympia is the most prestigious competition in bodybuilding. Only the best athletes in the world compete. Stepping onto that stage is a big accomplishment that many bodybuilders want to achieve but few actually do it. Dauda had a wonderful time, both personally and professionally. The first thing that stands out about competing at Olympia is the atmosphere. The Olympia's history, popularity, and energy set it apart from other bodybuilding events. The lights, the crowd, and the presence of bodybuilding legends all contribute to a setting where every competitor knows they are part of something bigger than just a contest. Dauda goes to the Olympia stage and sees fans from all over the world and famous athletes. This realisation makes things more difficult and exciting. Preparing for the Olympia stage takes months or years. Dauda has trained, eaten well, and mentally prepared before stepping onto that stage. His aim is to prove his

SAMSON DAUDA

world-class credentials. At the Olympia, every detail matters, from muscle conditioning to posing routines. Dauda knows that competing at this level means pushing his body to its limits and fine-tuning every aspect of his performance. One of the most important parts of competing at Olympia is the mental challenge. The pressure to perform at the highest level is huge, and the stakes are high. For Dauda, it's important to keep your mind clear and focused. Athletes can get nervous when they have to prepare for a competition. But Dauda's ability to stay calm and composed under pressure is one of the key factors that have allowed him to compete at this level. He utilises mental imagery and affirmations to maintain focus on his tasks. Dauda's ability to pose is also important on the Olympia stage. In bodybuilding competitions, posing plays a crucial role, significantly impacting a competitor's chances at the Olympia. Dauda has practised posing for a long time to make sure each pose shows what he is proficient at and what he needs to improve. On stage, he needs to move quickly and confidently, showing off his body in the best way possible.

SAMSON DAUDA

The judges look for a combination of muscle size, symmetry, and conditioning, but how an athlete looks is just as important. His Olympia success depends on his posing skills, which he has honed through practice and experience. Another important aspect of competing at Olympia is the camaraderie among athletes. Although bodybuilding is an individual sport, the shared experience of preparing for a high-level competition creates a sense of respect among competitors. Dauda finds it humbling and inspiring to be backstage with the best bodybuilders in the world. The athletes push each other to do their best, knowing that each competitor has gone through the same tough process to get there. This camaraderie doesn't make the event less competitive, but it adds a level of respect and sportsmanship that is unique to bodybuilding at this level. The Olympia is more than just a competition. Dauda has the chance to connect with his global fan base by competing on this stage. The Olympia draws bodybuilding enthusiasts from all over the world. Many of them follow Dauda's career closely. These fans like to see their favourite competitors on the Olympia stage. Dauda finds it exciting and motivating to perform in front of such a passionate and knowledgeable crowd. It reminds him why he started bodybuilding and how far he has come since then. Even though the competition is tough, Dauda enjoys competing at Olympia. It is the culmination of years of work, sacrifice, and dedication. Every time he steps on that stage, it's a chance to show the judges and fans, as well as himself, that he's one of the best in the world. The Olympia experience is a validation of his hard work and a reminder of what is possible when discipline and passion come together. Dauda thinks that the Olympia is more than just a competition. From the beginning of his bodybuilding career, the goal was always to compete on this stage. Even though it's stressful and lengthy, it's also a reward for the hard work he's done for many years. Dauda continues to push himself and leave his mark on the sport he loves.

Learning from Rival Competitors

SAMSON DAUDA

Samson Dauda has learned from rival bodybuilders that she should become a professional bodybuilder. Bodybuilding is a very competitive sport. The best athletes learn from each other and use their competitions to improve themselves. Observing and adapting lessons from his peers has marked Dauda's career. This has helped him grow in the sport. Learning from rivals is important because it helps you recognize their strengths and find ways to improve yourself. Dauda studies his competitors' bodies and workouts carefully. At major competitions like the Arnold Classic or Mr. Olympia, he is up against the best bodybuilders in the world, each with their own set of strengths. Dauda takes note of certain elements, such as muscle mass, symmetry, or conditioning. Dauda can think about ways to improve himself by watching how others train or practise their poses. Dauda also knows how important it is to keep up with industry trends. Bodybuilding is always changing, with new training techniques, diets, and poses coming out every year. Dauda knows that being his best requires more than doing what worked before. By watching rivals introduce new methods, he learns which ones are effective and how he could use them in his routine. Dauda is open to learning from his competitors. Dauda learns about bodybuilding by watching how competitors handle their emotions. Top competitors often come up with unique mental strategies to deal with stress and nerves. Dauda learns how experienced bodybuilders keep their cool under pressure and stay focused before a big competition. This helps her understand the mental strength needed to compete well. These lessons help him think better and stay calm when there is a lot of competition. Dauda learned a lot about how other companies handle problems. Every athlete faces challenges such as injuries, poor performance, or difficulty in gaining strength.

Dauda finds inspiration in his competitors' ability to overcome these challenges. He has learned that resilience is important in bodybuilding and that watching his competitors persevere through tough times reminds him that setbacks are temporary and can be overcome with determination and the right approach. This way of thinking has helped him stay focused even when things

SAMSON DAUDA

don't go as planned. He knows that learning from mistakes can make him stronger in the future. Dauda has an important opportunity to improve his competitive strategies. Each competitor has their own style, and learning how other competitors do their routines can give Dauda new ideas for improving his own. Watching his competitors perform helps him think about his own routine and try new things to show what he's talented at. The best competitors taught Dauda how to perform at his best when it counts. Dauda also understands the significance of maintaining mutual respect among competitors. In bodybuilding, people fight hard, but they also admire each other for their hard work. Dauda has learned that competing against the best makes him a better athlete, and he has accepted the idea that rival competitors are not only enemies but also sources of motivation. Dauda has to constantly improve his physique and approach to competing in events like Mr. Olympia. Dauda learned from his competitors by copying their methods and adapting those lessons to fit his own path. Each competitor has their own story, and Dauda finds value in understanding these stories. By thinking about how his rivals have reached the top of the sport, he gains perspective on his own journey and what he will need to do to reach his long-term goals. Samson Learning from other bodybuilders has shaped Dauda's approach to bodybuilding. Dauda has learned from those who challenge him on stage. He continues to improve as an athlete through careful observation, mental discipline, and mutual respect.

Balancing Fame and Focus

Samson Dauda's rise in professional bodybuilding is one of the most meteoric in recent competitive history. Dauda, also known as "The Nigerian Lion," became very popular in the IFBB Pro League after finishing second at the 2023 Mr. Olympia. Dauda has been training in the UK since he was young. His journey took a big turn when he got his pro card in 2018. He quickly became a strong competitor, unlike many athletes who take years to become successful. He improved his body slowly but surely with each competition appearance. Dauda started working with bodybuilding coach Milos Sarcev in 2022.

SAMSON DAUDA

This partnership led to significant improvements in his physique, particularly in terms of conditioning and overall appearance. People who covered bodybuilding noticed Dauda's performance in important shows. Dauda's combination of mass and aesthetics is what sets him apart. Despite his height and weight of around 290 pounds, Dauda maintains a good appearance and balance. Experts in bodybuilding and other competitors have praised his impressive back development. Dauda has kept focusing on his career as his profile has grown. Despite increasing media attention and a growing social following, he's kept his training environment relatively unchanged. He continues to train at his regular gym in the UK, choosing familiarity and consistency over more famous training facilities. In interviews, Dauda often talks about how important it is to stay grounded, even though he has become famous quickly. He has discussed his approach to balancing the demands of professional bodybuilding with his personal life, maintaining strong connections with his family and long-time training partners who have known him before his success in the sport. Dauda won the Arnold Classic in 2023. Winning

SAMSON DAUDA

one of the most prestigious titles in bodybuilding validated his potential and made him more visible. Instead of letting this success change his approach, Dauda changed his training methods and preparation strategies. His approach to social media and public presence shows a measured understanding of fame's double-edged nature. Dauda shares training tips and competition updates, but he keeps his personal life private. This helps him talk to fans and still stay focused for tough games. Dauda mixes old-fashioned training with modern science. He's known for his methodical approach to workouts, focusing on the mind-muscle connection instead of just moving heavy weights. He pays close attention to how he eats and recovers, and he's willing to try new things while sticking to the basics that work for him. The bodybuilding community has noted Dauda's ability to make improvements between shows, even when they are close to each other. This skill shows not only his genetics and work ethic but also his team's ability to make adjustments to his preparation plan. As bodybuilding continues to change, Dauda represents a balanced approach to modern professional athletics. He

SAMSON DAUDA

works on the business side of the sport, but he still works hard to compete at the highest level. His impact on bodybuilding goes beyond his achievements in competition. Dauda has become an inspiration for aspiring athletes, especially those from regions traditionally underrepresented in professional bodybuilding. He has demonstrated that anyone, with the right dedication and guidance, can build elite-level physiques anywhere. Dauda has shown that success doesn't always require changing one's approach or values. His ability to handle more attention and keep working on getting better has become a model for other athletes in the sport.

CHAPTER 7: The Role of Support Systems

Samson Dauda's support system is a complex network of professionals, family members, and trusted advisors who work together to help him succeed. This complicated system goes beyond the traditional coach-athlete relationship and covers many aspects of a competitor's career and personal life. Dauda's relationship with coach Milos Sarcev has been key to his competitive career. Sarcev is known for his scientific approach to bodybuilding preparation. He is a former professional bodybuilder and a coach to many elite athletes. This coaching relationship shows how important it is to have experienced help in the tough world of professional bodybuilding. Family support is important in Dauda's story. His wife has been a constant presence throughout his career progression, taking care of daily life and keeping him focused. This family foundation helps athletes succeed at the highest level. Training partners are another part of the support system. Dauda's training

SAMSON DAUDA

partners at his home gym in the UK have stayed the same since he became famous. These individuals not only help with training sessions but also keep a sense of normalcy and authenticity in a high-pressure environment. Training partners who know an athlete's journey from the beginning are very important. The medical team plays a crucial role in supporting professional bodybuilders. Keeping track of your health—like checking your bloodwork and looking at your body—requires healthcare professionals who know what the sport requires. These doctors make sure that getting fit and strong doesn't hurt your health in the long run. Nutritionists and meal preparation services are important in keeping elite bodybuilders on the right diet. Dauda requires extensive nutrition during his competition preparation. This part of support includes timing, food quality, and adjustments based on physiological responses. The business side of professional bodybuilding requires another layer of support. Managers, agents, and lawyers help with sponsorship deals, competition contracts, and other business opportunities that come with being successful in sports. This helps athletes focus on their training while taking care of their business needs. Mental health support is becoming more important in professional bodybuilding. Being very competitive, managing what others expect, and being very fit can make you feel very stressed. Access to mental health professionals who understand the unique challenges of elite bodybuilding has become an important part of comprehensive athlete support. Social media management and public relations are another important part of modern professional bodybuilding. Dauda takes a measured approach to social media, but having help with managing these platforms and public appearances helps keep a balance between public engagement and personal focus.

This aspect of support helps athletes navigate the modern landscape of professional sports while keeping their time and energy safe. Recovery specialists, such as physiotherapists, massage therapists, and other bodywork professionals, are important for keeping athletes healthy and preventing injuries. Bodybuilding requires regular body maintenance and injury prevention work, so these professionals are important members of the support team. The bodybuilding community, including fellow competitors and industry veterans, provides another layer of support through shared experiences and advice. This community aspect helps athletes deal with common challenges and stay positive throughout their competitive careers. The relationships formed in the professional bodybuilding community often offer valuable insights and opportunities for growth. Supplement companies and equipment manufacturers often become part of an athlete's support system through sponsorship relationships. These partnerships provide resources while also giving athletes the chance to contribute to product development and testing. This helps both the athlete and the industry as a whole. Having teams to assist with posing and tanning is crucial during show preparation. These individuals assist athletes in achieving their best on stage. They do this by preparing them for months. These specialists can make a big difference in the outcome of a competition. Gym owners and staff often play an important role in an athlete's support system. It's important to have good training facilities and a manager who can handle the unique needs of professional bodybuilding preparation. The role of photographers and videographers has become more important in modern bodybuilding. These professionals assist athletes in monitoring their progress, creating content for sponsors, and maintaining their public presence. Their work contributes to both the artistic and business aspects of an athlete's career. Financial advisors help athletes manage their money and make plans for the future. This help is very important for professional bodybuilders who need to think about their future after they finish competing. Online communities and fan groups can help motivate and encourage people during difficult times when they're preparing. Managing these relationships through the right channels helps athletes connect with their supporters while keeping their focus and energy. A support system's effectiveness often lies in its ability to work together while keeping clear boundaries and communication channels. Each member of the support network must understand how their role fits into the bigger picture of an athlete's career and well-being. This comprehensive approach to helping athletes becomes more important as the sport of bodybuilding gets better and more professional.

Family, Friends, and Personal Relationships

Samson Dauda's journey in professional bodybuilding is deeply connected to his personal relationships, which have played a crucial role in shaping both his career and character. He has kept strong connections with family and friends who knew him before his success in professional bodybuilding. Dauda's wife has been a constant source of support throughout his bodybuilding career. Their relationship goes beyond emotional support. She assists him with daily tasks that enable him to concentrate on winning big games. In interviews, Dauda said that his wife knows about the sport and is willing to change their lifestyle to fit his competition schedule. This has helped him succeed. The Nigerian athlete has greatly influenced his lifestyle and approach to sports. Dauda grew up in a family-oriented culture and has carried these values into his work. He keeps in touch with his family, who have helped him achieve his

SAMSON DAUDA

bodybuilding goals from the beginning. This group of families has helped keep things stable during tough times in professional sports. Dauda's relationship with his children adds another dimension to his life. Being an elite athlete and a father requires careful time management. He said that being a dad makes him want to do well but also helps him stay grounded and focused on what's most important. Dauda has built a close circle of friends in the UK. Dauda formed many of these relationships before his professional success, ensuring authentic connections unaffected by his growing fame. Friendships can give athletes a sense of normalcy and perspective that can be helpful when they're competing well. His friends in his gym at home in the UK are like family to him. Dauda stays with the same training group throughout their career. These individuals have witnessed Dauda's development into a highly skilled bodybuilder, and they share many similarities. Milos Sarcev, his coach, has become more than just an athlete and coach. Their relationship started in 2022, and they treat each other well. Sarcev has become a trusted advisor in Dauda's career and life decisions. Dauda has made friends with other bodybuilders outside of the sport. Shared experiences and a mutual understanding of the unique challenges faced by elite bodybuilders form the foundation of these relationships. Even though the sport is very competitive, friends can help each other and make friends. He approaches new relationships with a careful balance between being open and keeping boundaries.

Dauda has shown that success can attract different types of attention and has been selective in growing his inner circle. Dauda's original gym community in the UK is still important in his life. His friendships and support from his early training days are still strong. These people knew him before he became a professional and helped him stay connected to his roots in the sport. Dauda is also involved in the community. He has kept in touch with aspiring bodybuilders and athletes, especially those from similar backgrounds, offering advice and inspiration. These relationships allow him to give back to the community and stay connected to the grassroots level of the sport. The management of personal

SAMSON DAUDA

relationships while keeping a professional career requires careful balance. Dauda says he must set boundaries and manage time to prioritise his competitive goals and personal relationships. This approach has helped him stay connected while he works hard at his sport. His online presence lets people see his personal life, but he keeps his information private. Through these platforms, he shares moments with his family and friends. This measured approach to public sharing helps him keep his personal relationships with fans and followers authentic. These close friends have been very helpful during difficult times in his job. When you're getting ready for a competition, recovering from injuries, or dealing with high-level competition, having supportive friends can help you feel calm and give you practical help when you need it. These relationships have helped Dauda stay grounded even though he has grown quickly in the sport. Family, friends, and long-term associates help keep things in perspective and provide a support system that goes beyond bodybuilding competition.

SAMSON DAUDA

The Importance of Coaches and Mentors

Samson Dauda's bodybuilding career needed coaches and mentors, which shows how important it is to have experienced help in sports. His partnership with renowned coach Milos Sarcev, which began in 2022, was a turning point in his competitive journey. Sarcev has had a lot of influence on Dauda's development. Sarcev used to compete in bodybuilding and is currently a coach. He has a lot of experience and knows a lot about science. This approach has helped Dauda prepare for competitions and improve her presentations. The coaching relationship between Dauda and Sarcev shows how important chemistry is in athlete-coach partnerships. Their collaboration has led to significant improvements in Dauda's physique, especially in terms of conditioning and overall appearance. Dauda's success at the Arnold Classic and Mr. Olympia shows how successful this partnership is. Dauda has also had the help of various specialist coaches who focus on specific aspects of professional bodybuilding. Posing coaches have assisted Dauda in enhancing his stage presence, ensuring a well-presented physique during competitions. This extra help has helped him do better on stage. A mentor-mentee relationship in bodybuilding often goes beyond physical training and competition preparation. Expert mentors assist athletes in managing their careers and handling the business aspects of professional bodybuilding. This includes helping you find sponsors, promoting yourself, and planning your future career. Coaches and bodybuilders in the UK helped Dauda, recognizing his potential. These early coaches helped him learn about the sport and taught him important rules that still influence how he trains and prepares. Dauda's training method shows that it's important to have different perspectives on an athlete's growth. He has shown that he can combine knowledge from different sources, including other experienced professionals in the industry. He has made rapid progress because he is willing to learn and stays true to his beliefs. Nutrition coaches have helped Dauda grow and prepare for competitions. Professional bodybuilding nutrition requires expert advice to achieve and keep elite fitness levels. In professional bodybuilding, coaches and

SAMSON DAUDA

athletes need to talk constantly and adjust. Dauda's success shows how important it is to have coaches who can understand what athletes need physically and mentally and make changes as they get ready. Mental preparation and psychological coaching are becoming more important in professional bodybuilding. Mentors help athletes become strong enough to handle tough situations and stay focused during long training sessions. During competition peak week, experienced guidance can make a big difference in an athlete's final presentation. Having coaches who understand contest preparation helps athletes navigate this important period well. Dauda balances respect for authority with keeping his own identity as an athlete. He has kept his unique characteristics and style while following his coaches' advice. This shows how effective coaching enhances rather than changes an athlete's natural abilities. Technological advances have made it possible to monitor and adjust training and nutrition protocols more precisely. Dauda's coaching team uses tools and methods to keep track of progress and make data-driven decisions. The coaching network includes experts in recovering from injuries and preventing them from happening again. These professionals help keep you in excellent physical condition while preventing setbacks that could stop you from moving forward. Under their guidance, you can maintain intense training protocols for an extended period. Good coaching can help you grow professionally and stay in your job for a long time. Experienced mentors help athletes make decisions that balance competitive success with long-term health and career longevity. Coaching relationships enable coaches to impart their knowledge to the upcoming generation of athletes. Mentoring is a traditional method of maintaining and enhancing bodybuilding knowledge.

Sponsorships and Industry Partnerships

Samson Strategic partnerships and sponsorships have accompanied Dauda's rise in professional bodybuilding, demonstrating his competitive success and marketability in the industry. His approach to business relationships shows a careful balance between keeping authentic connections with brands while focusing on his

SAMSON DAUDA

competitive career. Dragon Pharma, a well-known supplement company, is one of Dauda's main sponsors. This relationship has grown with his success, giving him both financial and product support. The partnership shows how elite athletes can work with brands that match their professional goals and keep their credibility in the sport. He got more sponsors after winning big competitions. The second-place finish at the 2023 Mr. Olympia and victory at Arnold Classic made him more visible and valuable to potential sponsors, which led to more opportunities in the industry. Dauda only partners with companies that share his values and professional standards. This careful way of choosing sponsors has helped him stay popular with bodybuilders and make favourable business connections. Equipment partnerships are important for his training regimen. These relationships often involve working with manufacturers to test and give feedback on products, contributing to product development while ensuring access to high-quality training equipment. These partnerships help both athletes and the industry by creating new training equipment. Dauda's professional portfolio has become more important because of clothing and apparel sponsorships. These partnerships go beyond just letting people endorse products. They also help make products better and better for bodybuilders. His social media presence is a beneficial way for him to connect with sponsors and show products and services to his growing following. Dauda keeps a balance between promotional obligations and training content, which helps keep his brand partnerships authentic. Dauda can represent his sponsors at industry events and expos while connecting with fans and potential business partners. These appearances help build his personal brand in the bodybuilding community. The evolution of his sponsorship portfolio shows how important timing and strategic partner selection are in professional bodybuilding. As his competitive achievements have grown, so has his ability to choose sponsorship opportunities that match his long-term goals. Dauda's scientific approach to training and nutrition adds credibility to supplement companies when endorsed by an athlete known for his methodical preparation methods. This alignment between athlete methodology

SAMSON DAUDA

and sponsor values makes these partnerships more real. Dauda's work relationships with the media are becoming more important. Collaborations with bodybuilding media outlets and content creators help show his journey while giving his sponsors and partners exposure. Dauda is an athlete from Nigeria who competes in the UK. This makes her attractive to sponsors around the world. He can work with companies in different countries and still use the same brand message. His association with gyms is a crucial aspect of his professional relationships. These arrangements often provide important training environments while creating opportunities to promote each other. Partnerships with photographers and videographers are important for documenting Dauda's journey and creating content for sponsors. These partnerships help athletes and business partners keep a professional image while providing valuable marketing materials. Managing these different partnerships requires careful planning to make sure everyone does what they need to do without sacrificing training or getting ready for competitions. This balance shows how important it is to have effective help systems in place to handle business relationships well. As Dauda's career has progressed, financial services partnerships have become more important. They help him manage his professional earnings and investments. These relationships are important for planning and security in the long run. Dauda has always focused on partnerships that help him perform at the highest level while building sustainable business relationships. This way of doing things has helped him do well in both his job and business. His partnership portfolio has changed a lot in professional bodybuilding, where athletes have to balance traditional sponsorship models with new opportunities in digital media and direct-to-consumer marketing. Dauda's ability to adjust to these changes while keeping strong relationships shows how modern sports are always changing.

Fans and Community: How They Fuel His Success

Samson Dauda's relationship with his fans and the bodybuilding community is a unique part of his

SAMSON DAUDA

professional success. The Nigerian Lion has a passionate following that goes beyond typical fan support and creates a community that actively participates in his journey. Social media has helped fans connect with each other. Dauda posts regular updates on Instagram about how he trains, prepares, and competes. His approach to social media engagement is authentic and often gives real insights into the life of a professional bodybuilder while keeping professional boundaries. The UK bodybuilding community has been very supportive of Dauda's journey. Local gym members and other athletes who have seen him go from amateur to elite professional status provide a foundation of support that goes back before his international success. This grassroots backing has stayed strong even as his profile has grown globally. His appeal to fans comes from his rapid rise in the sport, which many find inspirational. The story of how he went from earning his pro card in 2018 to placing second at the Mr. Olympia in 2023 is inspiring for bodybuilders and fans who appreciate the hard work it takes to achieve this. Fans can follow this story and relate to it. The Nigerian diaspora community has embraced Dauda. His

SAMSON DAUDA

success has inspired many African athletes and fans. This connection to his heritage has helped him build a fan base that is diverse and passionate. Dauda's interactions with fans at expos and competitions show how important the community is to the sport. He's known for taking time to talk to supporters, answer questions, and share insight about training and preparation. These personal interactions help athletes and fans connect with each other and grow the sport. Fans have shown a lot of support for Daudas appearances at competitions.

This energy from the audience often helps athletes perform better when they need it most. Through social media, fans have been able to follow Dauda's physical transformation. He is open about his successes and failures, which fans like. This openness has helped build trust and credibility among the bodybuilding community. The bodybuilding media community has documented Dauda's journey. News and videos have shown his personality and how he plays the sport, making fans feel more connected to his journey. Fans have become a big

SAMSON DAUDA

part of the gym communities where Dauda trains. Instead of seeking isolation, he has kept an accessible presence in these environments, allowing fans to see his work ethic firsthand while respecting his training focus. He shares knowledge and experience with bodybuilders who want to become bodybuilders. Dauda helps people who want to look better by posting on social media, going to the gym, or appearing in person. Fans have shown their support at major competitions. The increasing number of people who support "Team Dauda" at shows indicates that fans are now supporting each other as a group. This collective support creates an atmosphere that can improve competitive performance. Dauda's relationship with the bodybuilding community extends to his relationships with other competitors. He treats competition and sports well, which has earned him the respect of his peers and fans. This has made the sport more positive. The internet lets fans follow Dauda's preparations in excellent detail. Fans can keep track of how he's doing, how he trains, and when he'll compete. This helps them become more involved and knowledgeable about elite bodybuilding. Community help is crucial when preparing for competitions. Fans sending encouraging messages during difficult training or preparations for competition can give extra motivation and emotional support when needed. Dauda's fan base has grown as more people around the world are interested in professional bodybuilding. His appeal to different audiences has helped the sport grow and expand. This shows how athletes can influence the sport by connecting with fans.

SAMSON DAUDA

CHAPTER 8: Challenges Along the Way

Samson Dauda's journey to become a professional bodybuilder has been difficult because he had to overcome many obstacles that tested his strength and determination. He has faced and overcome many obstacles that have shaped his approach to competition and professional development. One challenge early on was establishing himself as a Nigerian-born athlete in the UK bodybuilding scene. Breaking into professional sports in a new country is tough, from making connections in the industry to adapting to different training environments and competitive standards. Dauda had to adjust to new cultures and jobs while pursuing his bodybuilding goals. The financial demands of professional bodybuilding posed another substantial challenge during his early career. The cost of maintaining the necessary diet, supplementation, and training regimen required for elite competition can be considerable. Before securing major sponsorships, Dauda had to balance these expenses with everyday living costs, demonstrating the economic challenges

SAMSON DAUDA

faced by rising athletes in the sport. Physical transformation presented its own set of challenges. Dauda's journey to building and maintaining his competitive physique required careful management of his body's response to training and nutrition. The process of adding quality muscle mass while maintaining the aesthetics and conditioning required for professional competition demanded constant adjustments and attention to detail. Sometimes professional preparation has led to physical setbacks. Dauda has had to deal with injuries from training and physical stress while still competing. These challenges required careful balancing between progress and recovery. The transition from amateur to professional status was difficult. The increased competition level and expectations at the professional level made it necessary to change his training and preparation methods. Pro competition required quick adaptation to new standards and presentation requirements. He has had trouble managing his time during his career. Bodybuilding requires careful planning and prioritisation. As he became more successful, sponsors, media, and fans demanded more

SAMSON DAUDA

time from him. The mental pressure of competing at the highest level is challenging. As Dauda's profile has grown, so have expectations and scrutiny. Keeping calm and focused on preparing and performing requires a lot of mental strength. Travel and logistics have been challenging for an international athlete. Competing across different countries and continents requires careful planning for travel, accommodation, and training and nutrition protocols while away from home in the UK. Dauda faced unique challenges during the COVID-19 pandemic. The disruption to normal training routines, competition schedules, and access to facilities required adaptation and creativity to stay competitive during uncertain times. He had to overcome language and communication problems, especially when he was starting out in his career. Although fluent in English, it took extra effort and adaptation to navigate the specific terminology and cultural nuances of professional bodybuilding in different regions. The challenge of keeping progress while avoiding plateaus has required constant innovation in training and nutrition approaches.

SAMSON DAUDA

He has worked with coaches to find new ways to grow and improve while avoiding stagnation throughout his career. Meeting the needs of his sponsors and business partners while staying true to his own brand and beliefs has been difficult. It takes careful planning to balance commercial obligations with competitive preparation. The physical demands of keeping up with multiple shows in a row have tested his body's ability to recover. The 2023 season showed how difficult it is to perform at a high level across major competitions while managing recovery and preparation time. The food he consumes has been challenging because he requires a high calorie intake to maintain his health and consume quality food. The practical aspects of food preparation and consumption at this level present daily challenges that need careful planning and execution. The pressure of representing multiple communities adds another layer of responsibility and challenge. To keep in touch with different groups and reach your goals, you need to be careful and focused. Changes in judging criteria and presentation standards have required constant learning and adjustment. Professional bodybuilding is always changing, so athletes need to keep up with the latest trends and expectations while still being themselves and having their own unique qualities and abilities. It's important to create and keep a system that can handle the demands of elite competition. A team of coaches, nutritionists, healthcare providers, and business managers requires a lot of work and resource management. Personal sacrifice has been a theme throughout his journey. The dedication required for elite bodybuilding often means missing important family events, social gatherings, and other normal life events. Staying motivated and focused while making these sacrifices is a constant challenge. The rapid nature of his rise in the sport has also presented challenges in terms of managing expectations and keeping perspective. To keep getting better and doing better, you need to take care of your body and mind.

Injury and Recovery: Overcoming Setbacks

Samson Dauda is a bodybuilder who knows how to avoid injuries and recover from them. He knows that it's important to manage physical stress when competing at a certain weight and size. His experience shows that it's important to balance intense training with beneficial ways to recover. Training at the elite level, especially when you weigh around 290 pounds, puts a lot of pressure on the body's joints and connective tissues. Dauda has found a way to prevent injuries by paying close attention to how she lifts weights. His work with coach Milos Sarcev has made it more important to prevent injuries. Their training method emphasises controlled movements and proper execution over just moving heavy weights. This helps minimise the risk of training-related injuries while still giving you the necessary stimulus for growth and development. Dauda's training approach includes recovery protocols. He uses regular massage therapy, physiotherapy sessions, and rest periods between training sessions to recover. This comprehensive recovery plan helps bodybuilders recover from the intense physical demands of professional bodybuilding. Managing minor injuries and physical setbacks has been important for keeping progress consistent. Instead of pushing through pain, which could cause more serious injuries, Dauda is willing to change how he trains. He works around his limitations while still progressing overall. Sleep quality and quantity have become more important parts of his recovery protocol. Dauda knows that proper rest is important for injury prevention and recovery, so he makes sleep a key part of his preparation. Nutrition is important for his injury prevention and recovery strategy. Enough nutrients, particularly protein, enable his body to withstand the rigorous training without suffering injuries. When he trains, he uses protective gear like belts, wraps, and other things to prevent injuries. This careful attention to proper support helps keep joints and connective tissues safe during heavy training sessions. Working with healthcare professionals, including sports medicine specialists and physical therapists, has been important in addressing any physical issues before they become serious injuries. Regular assessments and preventive treatments help keep his body working well despite the intense training.

The challenge of maintaining size while managing joint stress requires careful balance between training intensity

SAMSON DAUDA

and volume. Dauda's approach includes strategic deload periods and varying the training intensity to allow for proper recovery while keeping muscle mass. His experience has shown him how important it is to listen to his body's signals and respond appropriately to prevent minor issues from becoming major ones. This knowledge has helped him stay on track and avoid serious injuries that could stop his career from competing. Guest appearances and competitions require special recovery protocols. He must manage the stress of travelling, perform well, and stay healthy to avoid injuries. Hydration is important for his injury prevention strategy. Fluid balance helps keep joints healthy and muscles working well while reducing the risk of training-related injuries. Compression therapy, ice baths, and other techniques show how he keeps his physical health while pursuing elite-level performance. He does a lot of stretching and moving around to prevent injuries. Despite his large muscle mass, he moves freely to minimise the risk of injury and enhance his performance and appearance. The management of training volume shows awareness of the relationship between workload and injury risk. You can prevent overuse injuries and still make progress by adjusting the intensity and volume of your exercise. Stress management is crucial for injury prevention as it can hinder physical recovery and heighten the likelihood of injury. Dauda takes care of his mental health as part of his overall health plan. Communication with his coaching team about physical limitations and recovery needs shows how important it is to have proper help in managing injury risk. Talking openly helps adjust training plans to suit his body's response and recovery. After training for a long time, he learned how his body works and what it can't do. This helped him decide how intensely to train and when to rest. This knowledge is important for maintaining long-term health while pursuing competitive goals.

Dealing with Self-Doubt and Fear

Samson Dauda, known as "The Nigerian Lion," has emerged as one of bodybuilding's most compelling figures. Significant battles with self-doubt and fear have marked his journey. But it wasn't straightforward for her

SAMSON DAUDA

to become a professional bodybuilder. In his early competitive years, Dauda struggled with self-doubt that came from comparing himself to established pros. He initially wondered if he really belonged to the elite ranks of professional bodybuilding. During his transition from amateur to professional status, the stakes and expectations increased dramatically. Dauda battled with self-doubt during his preparation for the 2023 Arnold Classic. He struggled with doubt about his ability to stand alongside established champions. But this event proved to be a turning point as he took second place, showing that his fears were unfounded and that he could compete at the highest level. Dauda had to deal with the pressure of representing both Nigeria and the UK in professional bodybuilding. One of the few African athletes to reach elite status. He felt like he had to do a decent job and motivate others from similar backgrounds. Dauda has been very open about his struggles with pre competition anxiety, especially regarding his conditioning. In various interviews, he has said that the fear of not being lean enough or not presenting his best package on stage would sometimes

SAMSON DAUDA

affect his preparation and mental state. This honesty about his vulnerabilities has resonated with many athletes in the bodybuilding community who face similar challenges. Dauda felt anxious because professional bodybuilding requires her to be massive and get ready for competitions. Throughout his career, the constant pressure to improve while avoiding injuries and maintaining health has been a significant source of stress for Dauda. Dauda has worked with coaches and mentors to overcome his fears. Chris Aceto, a well-known bodybuilding coach, has helped him improve both physically and mentally. This has given him the confidence to do his best. This professional help has been instrumental in helping him prepare for competitions. Social media has helped Dauda deal with self-doubt.

It has allowed him to connect with fans and share his story, but it has also exposed him to constant comparison and criticism. Learning how to navigate this digital landscape while keeping his mind focused has been a process. In the 2024 season, Dauda's approach to fear

SAMSON DAUDA

and self-doubt changed a lot. His higher grades and recognition in the professional world have made him feel confident in himself. But he keeps a humble approach, acknowledging that dealing with these psychological challenges is a process rather than a fixed issue. Dauda has been able to overcome self-doubt thanks to training partners and gym communities. The support system he has built around himself, especially in his UK training base, has helped him through tough times. Dauda's journey has been about his ability to turn self-doubt into motivation. Instead of letting fear control him, he learned to use it to get better. He uses his emotions to train and prepare better. Dauda feels anxious and doubtful because of the money involved in bodybuilding. The need to succeed has added another layer of psychological pressure to his competitive career. Dauda has developed coping mechanisms to deal with pre-competition anxiety. These techniques include visualisation, meditation, and keeping in touch with his support team. These methods play a crucial role in his preparation, enabling him to maintain focus and confidence during crucial moments.

SAMSON DAUDA

Navigating the Politics of the Bodybuilding Industry

Samson Dauda knows a lot about politics in bodybuilding, and it's interesting to see how it works. Dauda is new to bodybuilding and has had to learn quickly how to deal with complicated relationships, sponsors, and competition. The Nigerian-born athlete's entry into the IFBB Pro League presented challenges. Dauda struggled to gain recognition due to his affiliation with non-traditional bodybuilding groups in America or Europe. Professionalism and respect have marked his approach to building relationships in the industry, helping him overcome his initial outsider status. Dauda has experienced a significant amount of sponsorship politics in her career. Unlike some athletes who quickly join big supplement companies, he initially kept his independence and looked at potential partnerships carefully. This measured approach to business relationships showed his understanding of the political dynamics in the industry and the importance of making strategic decisions instead of rushing them. His media

SAMSON DAUDA

relationships have contributed to Dauda's rise within the sport. He has shown outstanding skill in managing his public image and keeping his presentations authentic. He has always been honest and polite in his interviews and appearances, which helps him avoid controversial headlines that can happen to other athletes. Dauda has had to navigate the politics of professional bodybuilding carefully. Because the sport is subjective, it's important to have positive relationships with judges and officials, but without compromising honesty. Dauda has done this by focusing on his best package on stage while keeping professional courtesy off stage. Dauda has become a prominent figure within the UK bodybuilding scene, balancing the dual role of representing both his adopted home and his Nigerian heritage. This position has required him to deal with the expectations and interests of multiple communities while building his professional career. Gym affiliations and training partnerships have also influenced Dauda's career. His choices of training facilities and training partners have shaped his network in the industry. He keeps positive relationships with other gym members and avoids arguments about who

SAMSON DAUDA

owns what in the sport. Dauda has shown an ability to use social media politics in professional bodybuilding. He uses his online presence to build a strong following while avoiding the controversial social media disputes that often happen between competitors.

Dauda's political acumen has been essential for preparing for contests and fostering coaching relationships. His decision to work with established coaches while keeping his own voice in his preparation has shown that he can benefit from experienced guidance while still being able to be an athlete. Dauda has centred his career strategy on the politics of competition placement and show selection. He knows how important timing and momentum are in professional bodybuilding. This strategic approach has helped him build a reputation and rank within the sport. Dauda has handled post-competition politics well. He has kept a respectful tone while being honest about his experiences and aspirations. This approach has helped him keep positive relationships in the industry while still standing up for himself. The global politics of bodybuilding have complicated Dauda's career. He has had to deal with different expectations and responsibilities as an athlete who represents many different countries and cultures. His success in this area has helped pave the way for other international athletes in the sport. Dauda has planned out guest appearances and seminars, which often involve political decisions about whether to accept or decline. His choices in this area have helped him build his brand and keep positive relationships with the industry. Dauda has been careful about the politics of supplement company affiliations. He knows how to use endorsements and sponsorships to promote products he believes in. Dauda has used industry events and expo appearances to strengthen his position in the bodybuilding community. His work and involvement at these events have helped him make beneficial friends and avoid political problems that can happen.

The Battle with Consistency and Motivation

Samson His struggle with consistency and motivation has shaped Dauda's journey in professional

SAMSON DAUDA

bodybuilding. His knowledge helps athletes stay at their best all year round. In his early career, Dauda had a challenging time staying consistent. It was challenging to go from being an amateur to being a professional athlete. He struggled to keep track of his diet, exercise, and recovery while taking care of other things in his life. Dauda has had a challenging time keeping her nutrition consistent. Because he is naturally tall and needs a lot of energy, it's challenging for him to eat enough food every day. He has talked openly about the mental and physical toll of eating the right amount of calories every day. Dauda's development has been based on training consistency. The need to push through intense workouts has taken a lot of mental strength. His training style has changed over time. He now focuses on working hard for a long time instead of doing it only once or twice. Dauda has had a challenging time keeping consistent because of travel and guest appearances. As his popularity in the sport increased, he had to find ways to keep up with his workouts while also working in different places and times. Dauda's motivation has changed a lot throughout her career. He had to come up with different ways to stay

SAMSON DAUDA

focused and motivated, like setting small goals and finding new ideas. Dauda is motivated and consistent because of the money involved in professional bodybuilding. Dauda must generate income from various sources while preparing for competitions, which can hinder his ability to perform at his best. Dauda's family responsibilities and personal relationships have made it challenging for him to keep his preparation consistent. To balance life and bodybuilding, you need to plan carefully and sometimes make sacrifices. Daudas has faced numerous challenges that have tested his motivation. Dealing with injuries, managing recovery, and adapting to the body's changing needs have all taken a lot of attention and adjustment. Dauda has been fighting for consistency. The challenge of keeping up with demanding training and nutrition protocols has required careful planning and lifestyle changes. The weather and seasonal changes in the UK have significantly altered Daudas routine and motivation. To train during cold winters and eat healthy during different seasons, you need to plan ahead and be strong mentally. Dauda's training partners and support systems have been

SAMSON DAUDA

important in her quest for consistency. Having beneficial training partners who work as hard as him has helped him stay motivated during tough times. Dauda's consistency has been challenged by competition preparation. To achieve peak performance at certain times while still progressing overall, you need to carefully plan and adjust things like how hard you train, what you eat, and how you recover. Social media presence and public visibility have made Dauda's journey harder, which has affected his motivation both positively and negatively. The constant scrutiny of his body and progress has required mental resilience and the ability to stay focused on long-term goals. Dauda has learned from both successes and failures in her approach to consistency. He has been able to adapt and refine his methods based on experience. Cultural factors have influenced Daudas' relationship with consistency and motivation. His Nigerian background and UK residence have helped him develop a unique approach to bodybuilding. Dauda has been able to keep consistency by managing her time. Planning and prioritising multiple commitments has required careful planning. It's been

SAMSON DAUDA

challenging to stay motivated mentally and physically. Dauda has been working on strategies to overcome psychological barriers and keep focus during difficult times.

SAMSON DAUDA

CHAPTER 9: Inspiring the Next Generation of Athletes

Samson Dauda works to inspire and mentor the next generation of bodybuilding athletes. He approaches this role with authenticity, accessibility, and a genuine desire to share knowledge with aspiring competitors and fitness enthusiasts. Dauda regularly posts updates on his social media platforms about his training methods and preparation strategies. Instead of keeping his secrets, he shares how to exercise, eat healthy, and prepare mentally. This transparency has made him a valuable resource for young athletes who want to understand what professional bodybuilding is like. The Nigerian Lion's journey from a late start in bodybuilding to elite professional status resonates with young athletes who may feel they've missed their chance. Dauda believes that success in bodybuilding depends on hard work, staying consistent, and smart eating. In various interviews and guest appearances, Dauda always stresses the importance of education and proper guidance in

SAMSON DAUDA

bodybuilding. He stresses the importance of learning from experienced mentors and taking time to understand the basics before pursuing aggressive training and dietary protocols. This responsible approach to developing athletes has earned him respect from both veterans and newcomers in the sport.

Dauda is a bridge between different bodybuilding cultures in Africa and the United Kingdom. His success has made it easier for African athletes to compete in bodybuilding, showing that where you live or what your background is doesn't matter. He regularly meets with fans and athletes from these regions, offering advice and encouragement. Dauda mentors people through seminars and visits to gyms. These sessions often focus on mental aspects of competitive bodybuilding, such as setting goals, dealing with pressure, and keeping balance in one's life while pursuing athletic excellence. His presence on various bodybuilding podcasts and media outlets has allowed him to reach a wider audience with his message of dedication and professionalism in the sport. Dauda is a strong advocate for healthy training and

SAMSON DAUDA

nutrition practices that can help athletes develop long-term. Dauda has set a positive example as a professional athlete. His courteous behaviour, willingness to keep getting better, and ability to handle both wins and losses with grace have taught young athletes how they should act when competing. As a mentor, Dauda stresses the importance of patience and progressive development. He often tells stories about his own journey, including the challenges and setbacks he faced, helping to create realistic expectations among aspiring athletes about the time and effort it takes to succeed in professional bodybuilding. His way of getting ready for competitions has inspired many young athletes. Dauda's emphasis on maintaining a reasonable condition year-round has influenced how many young bodybuilders approach their own development. His guidance has a big impact on the business side of bodybuilding. Dauda talks about the importance of building a personal brand, keeping professional relationships, and creating opportunities that are beyond competition. This guidance helps young athletes get ready for a career in professional bodybuilding. Dauda encourages athletes to understand their bodies and find ways that work for them instead of just following others' methods. Mentoring has helped many athletes develop more sustainable and effective training and nutrition strategies.

Giving Back to the Bodybuilding Community

Samson Dauda has been a prominent figure in bodybuilding not only because of his competitive achievements, but also because of his important contributions to the bodybuilding community. His commitment to giving back shows in various ways. Dauda is very involved in the community because he regularly goes to gym seminars and workshops. These events help people who want to become bodybuilders learn from his experience. During these sessions, he talks about training techniques, nutrition, and the mental aspects of competitive bodybuilding. Dauda takes the time to address individual questions and concerns, giving personalised advice based on each participant's specific circumstances.

SAMSON DAUDA

The Nigerian Lion has been particularly active in supporting bodybuilding initiatives in both the United Kingdom and Africa. By connecting with local gyms and fitness communities in these areas, he helps create opportunities for athletes who might otherwise have a hard time getting high-level guidance and support. His presence at local competitions and events helps make these occasions better and inspire competitors of all levels.

Dauda has created a resource for bodybuilding knowledge through his social media platforms. He often posts detailed breakdowns of his training sessions, explaining how to choose exercises, refine techniques, and plan workouts. This content goes beyond simple workout demonstrations and explains why he chose them and how they fit into larger training goals.

Dauda helps young athletes develop by mentoring them. This coaching helps you prepare for competitions, practice posing, and deal with the stress of competing well. He thinks it's important to learn all the skills needed to be a good bodybuilder.

SAMSON DAUDA

Dauda's community involvement is especially important. He works with people who write about bodybuilding to make things that help everyone. These collaborations often result in detailed training guides, nutrition protocols, and competition preparation strategies that athletes can use at various stages of their development. Dauda's commitment to promoting health and safety in bodybuilding is clear in his public discussions about responsible approaches to the sport. He says it's important to keep getting stronger, getting enough rest, and being healthy while trying to build muscle. This message about being responsible helps stop some extreme ideas in the community.

Dauda has been generous with sharing his methods and experiences in terms of competition preparation. He regularly writes about how he prepares for major competitions and how he deals with the various challenges. This transparency helps new competitors understand the process and set realistic expectations about the dedication required to compete at a high level.

SAMSON DAUDA

His involvement in charity events and fundraising activities within the bodybuilding community shows his commitment to using his platform for good. Dauda often takes part in exhibitions and guest posing events where proceeds go to different causes. This helps to strengthen the connection between bodybuilding and community service.

Dauda's community work has also focused on building local bodybuilding scenes. He helps gym owners and event organisers create opportunities for bodybuilders to compete, especially in areas where the sport is still growing. He attends these events and helps make bodybuilding more popular in these areas.

Dauda works to create opportunities for other athletes. He uses his influence to help athletes connect with sponsors and opportunities.

Dauda also helps with professional development in bodybuilding. He shares insights about the business aspects of professional bodybuilding, helping other athletes build careers in the sport. This helps you create your own identity, use social media, and make extra money by competing with others.

SAMSON DAUDA

He also interacts with fans and supporters at expos and bodybuilding events. Dauda takes time to answer questions, pose for photos, and talk to bodybuilding enthusiasts. This accessibility helps break down barriers between professional athletes and amateur enthusiasts, which makes the community more inclusive.

Expanding His Brand Beyond Bodybuilding,

Samson Dauda has developed a brand that resonates with a variety of audiences. His approach to brand building combines his athletic accomplishments with business acumen and authentic engagement across various platforms. Dauda has grown its brand by using social media. Through platforms like Instagram and YouTube, he has cultivated a large following by sharing content that appeals to both hardcore bodybuilding enthusiasts and general fitness audiences. His content strategy combines competitive preparation insights with more accessible fitness and lifestyle content, helping him reach a wider audience beyond the competitive bodybuilding niche. The Nigerian Lion is now selling

SAMSON DAUDA

fitness clothes and working with well-known brands to make unique clothing lines. These collections often reflect his personal style while being useful for training. He is involved in the design process, making sure products meet the practical needs of serious athletes while appealing to casual fitness enthusiasts. Dauda has formed strong relationships with well-known companies in the supplement industry. He has taken an active role in product development and testing, giving advice based on his experience as an elite athlete. This hands-on approach has helped his brand and the products he endorses build credibility. Speaking has become another important part of Daudas brand expansion. He often speaks at fitness events, corporate wellness meetings, and motivational seminars. He can talk to people who might not normally be interested in bodybuilding competitions. This helps him reach more people and promotes the sport to new ones. Making digital content is an important part of Dauda's brand plan. He has made valuable digital assets through training videos, lifestyle vlogs, and educational content. This content helps audiences connect with him on a more personal level.

SAMSON DAUDA

Dauda has been able to make money while reaching a global client base with online coaching and training programs. These programs blend his expertise in bodybuilding with simple training techniques, catering to individuals with varying fitness levels. These programs maintain the quality of his guidance and enable him to reach a wider audience than just one-on-one coaching. Media presence has expanded through strategic appearances on podcasts, television shows, and digital platforms. These opportunities allow Dauda to share his story with diverse audiences while establishing himself as a thought leader in fitness and personal development. His articulate communication style and engaging personality make him an appealing guest for various media formats. The development of exclusive content through subscription-based platforms has created additional revenue streams while providing value to dedicated followers. Often, this content consists of detailed training programs, nutrition guides, and behind-the-scenes footage, appealing to serious enthusiasts who are willing to invest in premium content. Dauda has developed training courses and workshops as part of its brand extension. These programs often combine online learning with in-person components to create educational experiences that appeal to both aspiring bodybuilders and fitness professionals. Strategic partnerships have helped us expand internationally, especially in Africa and Europe. These relationships help him establish a brand presence in new markets while keeping his global image consistent. Cultural awareness and understanding of the local market have been key factors in successful international expansion. Dauda's business ventures in the health and wellness sector have allowed him to diversify his income streams while staying true to his core brand values. These efforts usually focus on making fitness and health more sustainable, which makes him more trustworthy than just competing in bodybuilding. Dauda continues to look for new ways to grow the brand. His ability to keep authentic connections while pursuing commercial opportunities has helped create a business model that lasts beyond his competitive career.

Shaping the Future of the Sport

SAMSON DAUDA

Samson Dauda has influenced the future of bodybuilding by doing different and trying new things. He has made a big difference by making bodybuilding more modern while still keeping its traditional values. Dauda has been instrumental in promoting a more sustainable approach to bodybuilding. He tries to stay in excellent shape all year round instead of changing weight a lot, which is healthier for the sport. This approach has started to influence how new competitors prepare for contests and off-season protocols. The Nigerian Lion has challenged traditional standards in professional bodybuilding. His ability to combine big size and attractive looks shows that other people can do the same thing. This balance has influenced the judgement of judges and the preparation of competitors, potentially enhancing the overall balance of the sport. Dauda is the first to combine modern sports science with traditional bodybuilding principles. His method uses the latest knowledge about how muscles work and how to recover while still keeping the basic principles of pushing yourself harder and harder that have been part of the sport for a long time. Dauda's professional image has helped make the sport more

SAMSON DAUDA

popular in mainstream fitness circles. He has shown that bodybuilders can be both physically impressive and intellectually engaged, helping to break down stereotypes that have limited the sport's appeal. Dauda is helping new bodybuilders become healthier by coaching and mentoring them. His emphasis on proper progression and sustainable development has influenced how athletes view their long-term development in the sport. Dauda has been a leader in using technology to prepare for contests. He uses advanced tools and analysis to prepare for competitions. This shows how modern tools can make traditional bodybuilding better. This integration helps modernise the sport while keeping its core principles. Dauda's influence on competition formatting and presentation is notable, especially how he approaches posing and stage presence. His style combines classical poses with modern presentation techniques to help competitors show off their bodies to audiences and judges. Dauda's success and advocacy helped shape bodybuilding in Africa. His achievements have helped African athletes get into professional bodybuilding, which could make the sport more diverse and popular around the world. Dauda talks about the sport's future in interviews and appearances in the news. He talks about how to make the sport more accessible to newcomers while keeping its competitive integrity. His approach to fan engagement and community building has helped create more interactive relationships between professional athletes.

This connection helps keep the sport relevant for new generations while creating stronger support systems for upcoming athletes. Dauda's open way of sharing his methods has made it easier for everyone to learn about the sport. Being open makes competition better and makes beneficial bodybuilding more accessible to people who want to do it. Dauda's example has also affected the business aspects of professional bodybuilding. His success in building a personal brand while being competitive shows future professionals how to make careers in the sport. Dauda contributes to the presentation of the sport to wider audiences. His ability to explain complicated training and nutrition ideas in easy-to-understand ways helps people who compete in

SAMSON DAUDA

bodybuilding and people who just like to exercise. Dauda's influence on competition standards extends to his advocacy for more objective judging criteria. His discussions about physique assessment and competition scoring help drive conversations about maintaining consistency and fairness in professional bodybuilding. The development of regional bodybuilding scenes has benefited from Dauda's support and guidance. His involvement in local competitions and exhibitions helps establish higher standards while creating more opportunities for upcoming athletes to develop their careers. His influence on training methods includes promoting more balanced approaches to muscle development. Instead of focusing only on size, Dauda emphasises the importance of proportion, detail, and overall aesthetic appeal. This could influence how future competitors approach their development. Dauda advocates for positive changes in how people see and do bodybuilding. His approach to competition, health, and professional development helps the sport grow.

CHAPTER 10: Looking Forward

Samson Dauda's career in bodybuilding is going through important changes that could affect it and the sport. His current position in the IFBB Pro League suggests that he has a bright future full of opportunities and challenges. Dauda has countless opportunities to further establish his dominance. With his strong performances at recent major competitions, including the Arnold Classic victory and strong Olympia performances, he has established himself as a serious contender for bodybuilding's most prestigious titles. His constant physical improvement and strategic approach to competition show that he hasn't yet reached his full potential. Dauda will keep improving his training in the future. His methodical approach to training techniques shows a commitment to continuous improvement. The way he trains and recovers shows that his body might get even better in the future. Dauda's forward strategy seems to include expanding its business. His growing presence in the fitness industry and successful partnerships with brands suggest the possibility of bigger business ventures. He could become

SAMSON DAUDA

more influential if he creates his own products, offers coaching services, and works with the media. Dauda has a lot of potential in the international market, especially in Africa and Europe. His position as an athlete with strong connections to multiple regions makes him a suitable fit to connect with different bodybuilding markets and cultures. This could make bodybuilding more influential in emerging markets. Dauda's future activities look to include more educational initiatives. He wants to share his knowledge and create comprehensive training programs. This could lead to more structured educational programs. This could include the creation of certification programs, training academies, or online education platforms. Dauda continues to focus on building communities. His engagement with fans and supporters through various platforms shows plans for stronger community development. This could include creating more interactive platforms for fan engagement, developing membership programs, or holding regular community events. Competition strategy refinement is important for Dauda's future success. He keeps changing how he prepares and presents for big contests, which could lead to new ideas. This entails improving his training and incorporating new elements into his poses.

Dauda wants to expand her media presence in the future. Dauda is becoming more adept at utilising various media platforms and public speaking, which could potentially lead to increased media exposure. This could include more mainstream media appearances or expanded digital content creation. Dauda uses technology in her training and preparation methods to help athletes grow. His willingness to use new training and monitoring technologies suggests a new approach to bodybuilding preparation and performance optimization. Mentorship program development could see growth in the coming years. Dauda's commitment to helping upcoming athletes suggests that mentorship programs could be more structured. This might include formal coaching programs, athlete development systems, or educational partnerships with fitness institutions. Dauda's future strategy seems to include brand diversification. His success in fitness-related markets suggests that the brand could expand into new areas. This could include items

SAMSON DAUDA

such as clothing, health-related services, or specialised training equipment. Strategic partnerships and collaborations show that the fitness industry can have a bigger impact. Dauda's growing network of professional relationships suggests opportunities for new projects and ventures that could change the direction of bodybuilding in the future. Dauda's forward momentum is based on building a competitive legacy. His consistent improvement and strategic approach to major competitions suggest that he will continue to pursue prestigious titles and achievements that could make him one of bodybuilding's elite competitors. Dauda appears to be concentrating on cultivating leadership within the industry. He's talking more about bodybuilding and helping athletes, so he might have more influence on what the industry does. Dauda's future plans will focus on improving her personal brand. His careful cultivation of a professional image and connection with audiences suggests potential for expanded influence across various platforms and markets. Dauda continues to prioritise athletic development in his forward strategy. His commitment to physical improvement and competitive excellence shows that he continues to push the limits of his physiological potential while keeping health and longevity in the sport. Dauda's future plan seems to focus on adapting to the market and innovating. He can figure out what's new in the industry and use it to help athletes and businesses grow.

Future Goals: Beyond the Stage

Samson Dauda, a professional bodybuilder, has become famous because of his dedication to the sport. As he continues to build his bodybuilding career, his goals go beyond the competition stage. Samson has always worked hard to be physically fit, but he wants to make a bigger impact in the future. Samson wants to use his platform to inspire young athletes in the future. He has stressed the importance of mentoring younger bodybuilders to help them meet the sport's challenges. He's passionate about sharing insights that help others avoid the mistakes he made early on. Samson wants to build a community where athletes can learn from each other and help bodybuilding grow and develop. Samson

SAMSON DAUDA

has expressed a strong interest in expanding his influence in the fitness industry. His success on stage has made him well-known, but he wants to use that to make more money in business, especially in areas like fitness classes, personal training, and health products. Samson is thrilled to continue his career and share his knowledge and love for fitness with more people. Dauda wants to help people reach their fitness goals through seminars, online coaching, and even making his own supplements. Samson's future goals revolve around promoting physical and mental wellness. Samson talked about how it's important to have a balance in life, especially between being physically fit and being mentally healthy. He wants to promote holistic well-being more actively in the coming years. Samson wants bodybuilding to become more than just looking appealing physically. He wants to work with wellness groups, give talks, and start wellness programs. His personal journey through the mental demands of competition has shaped his view of this and led him to advocate for mental health awareness in the fitness community. Samson has aspirations that go

SAMSON DAUDA

beyond bodybuilding. He has said that he wants to help the communities that have helped him in his career.

Samson wants to use his platform to make positive change. He has a strong desire to help others succeed, no matter where they start from. Samson is interested in helping others, and he wants to do this for a long time. Additionally, Samson understands the importance of maintaining a healthy lifestyle after competing in bodybuilding. He is still very focused on doing well in his competitions and continuing to make strides in the sport, but he is also realistic about the fact that a professional athletic career is limited. He wants to create a legacy that goes beyond bodybuilding. Samson wants to create opportunities that he can use long after he stops competing. He has expressed his interest in pursuing careers in media fields such as fitness broadcasting, commentary, or motivational speaking. Future goals for Samson Dauda also revolve around family and personal satisfaction. He has said that he wants to eventually settle down and focus on his family while still being involved in the fitness community. Samson's long-term plans often include a balance between professional ambition and personal satisfaction. He wants to make sure that as he succeeds in his professional endeavour, he also makes room for personal growth and family life. Samson Dauda's vision for the future is multifaceted and driven by a desire to impact the bodybuilding community and beyond. Samson wants to make a difference through mentoring, fitness, mental health, and giving back. He wants to continue to inspire and influence others beyond bodybuilding.

Life After Competition: What's Next for Samson Dauda?

As Samson Dauda's bodybuilding career continues to grow, the question of what life will be like for him after competition is important. Samson is known for his strong body and hard work. He has achieved important goals in the sport. But he knows that competitive bodybuilding is like any other professional athletic career. His predictions for the future demonstrate a broad perspective that extends beyond the fitness industry.

SAMSON DAUDA

Samson has always been interested in fitness and the principles of strength and discipline that bodybuilding requires. As he thinks about life after competition, one of his main goals is to stay involved in the fitness industry. He has said he would like to move into fitness coaching and mentoring. Samson has a lot of experience and knowledge from years of training and competing, and he wants to help the next generation of athletes by sharing strategies for both physical development and mental resilience. This mentorship would allow him to stay close to the sport that has shaped his life while helping future competitors. Samson said he wants to learn about fitness. He has dedicated himself to improving his craft throughout his career. He has often stressed the importance of proper training techniques, nutrition, and recovery. Samson wants to focus more on teaching others about bodybuilding and fitness in general. This could take the form of seminars, workshops, or even training programs that reach a large audience. His goal is to help people live healthier, more active lives. Samson is likely to explore the business side of the fitness industry. Over the years, many successful bodybuilders have started their own businesses. Samson believes this is a beneficial idea. He wants to start his own line of supplements, workout gear, or fitness brand that reflects his philosophy and commitment to excellence. With his established reputation and loyal fanbase, these ventures could allow him to build on his success and continue building on his legacy. Samson's life after bodybuilding will likely involve media and public speaking. He has the potential to work with bodybuilding organisations or media outlets to provide expert analysis and insights. This would keep him interested in the sport and give him new opportunities to improve. Samson could also use his story to inspire others. Samson's journey from a promising amateur to an elite competitor has been replete with obstacles, victories, and lessons that audiences beyond the bodybuilding world could apply. Samson prioritises personal growth alongside his professional aspirations.

Life after competition gives him the chance to explore his interests and passions. He plans to focus on family and personal fulfilment in the future. Samson has said

SAMSON DAUDA

that he wants to strike a better balance in the future. This could mean spending more time with loved ones, travelling, or doing hobbies and interests that he might have put off during his peak competitive years. Samson Dauda is interested in helping others, which is another area besides bodybuilding. He is passionate about giving back to communities and causes that resonate with him. This can happen through helping others, helping young people, or helping people who are not well-off. Samson's desire to make a positive difference in the world is a strong force, and he will likely spend more time and resources doing this. Samson's outlook on life after competition also shows a deeper understanding of the importance of mental and emotional well-being. Throughout his career, he has talked about how intense it is to be at the top of a physically demanding sport. In his post-competitive life, he plans to focus more on mental health. This could lead to collaborations with mental health organisations, sharing his own experiences, and helping others who are dealing with similar pressures. Samson wants to help people understand fitness and health in a more holistic way. Samson Dauda's vision for

SAMSON DAUDA

life after competition is about continuing his legacy while expanding into new and fulfilling roles. He plans to stay active in the fitness world, whether through business, coaching, philanthropy, or personal pursuits. He is determined, really wants to do well, and wants to inspire others. He will keep working hard even after he finishes competing.

The Evolution of His Training and Philosophy

Samson Dauda's evolution as a bodybuilder is more than just about his physical transformation. Samson's approach to training has changed over the years. This change shows that he is always improving his methods and trying new things. At first, Samson focused on building strength and muscle mass. Like many new athletes, he started with simple exercises like squats, deadlifts, and bench presses. These exercises helped him get stronger in his core, which is important for bodybuilding. Samson was mainly concerned with increasing the amount of weight he could lift. He knew that raw strength would be the foundation of his body.

SAMSON DAUDA

Samson began to realise that bodybuilding was more than just lifting heavy weights. This change in focus started his evolution from a strength-based approach to a more nuanced strategy that focused on muscle isolation and targeted development. He started to do more isolation exercises, focusing on specific muscle groups to create the look that bodybuilding is known for. Samsons workouts became more focused on form, time under tension, and muscle engagement instead of sheer power. Samuel changed how he exercises and how hard he trains. At first, he trained hard, hitting each muscle group multiple times a week with many sets and repetitions. Over time, he learned that it's important to recover and to use volume wisely. Samson began to train to grow while avoiding overtraining. By taking more rest days and changing the frequency with which he trained certain muscle groups, he allowed his body to recover and grow. Another important change in Samson's training philosophy was his approach to cardio. While many bodybuilders see cardio as a necessary evil, Samson has made it part of his year-round routine. He

SAMSON DAUDA

knows that cardiovascular health is important for both performance and longevity.

Samson has tried different types of cardio, like HIIT and steady-state, depending on what he wants to achieve in his career. Samson thinks nutrition is crucial when he trains, and his way of eating has changed a lot. At first, he focused on eating as many calories as possible to help his muscles grow. He mostly ate protein and carbohydrates. But as Samson got better at eating, he started paying more attention to timing his meals and changing the amount of food he eats to fit his training goals, whether he was getting bigger, losing weight, or staying healthy. Samson has changed how he thinks about training. During his youth, he primarily found motivation from external sources. He aspired to triumph in competitions, showcase his skills, and gain recognition within the bodybuilding community. As Samson's career has progressed, his motivation has become more internal. He has developed a deep love for the process of training itself—the discipline, the daily grind, and the pursuit of constant improvement. This

SAMSON DAUDA

shift in mindset has allowed him to stay focused and motivated, even during challenging times or when results on the stage were not immediate. Samson has been focusing on getting better and avoiding injuries as an athlete. At first, Samson didn't think about getting better. He kept working out even when he was exhausted and hurt. But as he gets older, he realises how important it is to rest, move around, and do things like stretching, foam rolling, and yoga to get better. Samson has been able to work longer and avoid injuries that could stop him from progressing. Samson Dauda's training and philosophy have changed over the course of his career. He keeps getting better as he trains harder, eats better, and stays focused mentally.

SAMSON DAUDA

CONCLUSION

Samson Dauda's success in bodybuilding shows that hard work, perseverance, and learning are important. Dauda has worked hard to improve his sport from his beginnings to competing at the Olympics. His intense workout regimens, focus on recovery, strategic use of supplementation, and unwavering mental toughness have all played key roles in his success. Dauda shows how to stay focused on long-term goals, deal with competition pressure, or see success.

Learning from rivals and accepting the challenges of elite competition have helped him grow both mentally and physically. Dauda has had the chance to show off his hard work and learn from the best athletes in the sport. A commitment to excellence that goes beyond individual competitions.

Samson Dauda is a model of what it takes to succeed at the highest level of bodybuilding. His job involves planning ahead, staying strong mentally, and being open to learning from different situations, like competition or personal difficulties. Dauda is a true champion who

SAMSON DAUDA

enjoys all aspects of sports and always strives to be the best.